NAPOLI TRAVEL GUIDE 2024

Napoli Unveiled: A Journey Through History, Culture, and Culinary Delights

STEVE BILLS

Copyright@ 2024 by Steve Bills

All rights are reserved. This book cannot be duplicated, distributed, or communicated without the publisher's prior written consent. This includes photocopying, recording, and other electronic or mechanical techniques.

TABLE OF CONTENT

TABLE OF CONTENT..2
INTRODUCTION...5
   About Napoli..6
   Why Napoli Is a Must-Visit Destination.....................8
CHAPTER 1: PLANNING YOUR TRIP TO NAPOLI... 10
   When to Visit Napoli... 10
   How to Get to Napoli...13
   Getting Around Napoli... 15
   Choosing the Right Accommodation...................... 17
   What to Pack.. 20
   Visa and Entry Requirements.................................23
   Currency and Language... 26
   Suggested Budget.. 27
   Money-Saving Tips... 30
   Best Places to Book Your Trip................................ 33
CHAPTER 2: GETTING TO KNOW NAPOLI.............. 37
   A Brief History of Napoli..38
   Understanding the History of Napoli....................... 39
CHAPTER 3: EXPLORING NAPOLI'S
NEIGHBORHOODS... 42
   Centro Storico...42
   Chiaia..45
   Vomero... 48
   Posillipo.. 51
   The Spanish Quarter.. 53
   SANITA... 56

CHAPTER 4: ICONIC LANDMARKS AND HIDDEN GEMS... 59
- Iconic Landmarks...59
- Castel Nuovo.. 61
- The Palazzo Reale Di Capodimonte......................64
- Spaccanapoli.. 69
- Via San Gregorio Armeno......................................71
- The Galleria Umberto I... 74

HIDDEN GEMS.. 76
- Fontenelle Cemetery.. 76
- Villa Floridana... 77
- Napoli Sotterranea (Underground)........................ 77
- The Santa Chiara Cloister..................................... 77
- Villa Doria D'Angri...77
- Sansevero Chapel (Calle Sansevero)................... 78

CHAPTER 5: MOUTHWATERING CUISINE AND DINING EXPERIENCES... 79
- Neapolitan Pizza..80
- Seafood specialist...82
- Street food Delights.. 84
- Dinner with a View.. 86
- Traditional Trattorias... 89

CHAPTER 6: ENGAGING CULTURAL EXPERIENCES. 90
- Artistic Treasures.. 92
- Sophisticated Treats... 94
- Bright Street Life... 97
- Cultural Festivals and Events................................ 98

CHAPTER 7: 7-DAY ITINERARY IN NAPOLI.......... 101

Day 1: Arrival and Historic Centre Exploration..... 101
Day 2: Artistic treasures and Castel dell'Ovo........102
Day 3: Pompeii and Herculaneum excursion........103
Day 4: Food Tour and Quartieri Spagnoli............. 103
Day 5: Capri Island Tour.. 104
Day 6: Vesuvius and Wine Tasting....................... 105
Day 7: Departure... 105
CHAPTER 8: Practical Information and Tips About Napoli..107
Etiquette and Customs.. 107
Simple Language Phrases to know in Napoli....... 110
Health and Safety Tips.. 113
Emergency Number... 116
Interactions and Web Connections....................... 118
Useful Apps and Websites.................................... 121
CONCLUSION..125

INTRODUCTION

In the scorching heat of a Mediterranean day, I set out on my first journey to Napoli, the throbbing center of southern Italy. With each stride along its winding lanes, I found a city brimming with vivid energy and centuries of history interlaced into its cobblestones.

Napoli welcomed me with its wild appeal as soon as I got off the train. The perfume of freshly baked sfogliatella mixed with the salty wind from the neighboring sea, compelling me to explore further into its crowded lanes.

Wandering around the historic center, I was struck by the grandeur of Piazza del Plebiscito, where the majestic exterior of the Royal Palace stood in sharp contrast to the bustling street entertainers and merchants peddling their products.

As I continued on, the ancient ruins of Pompeii and Herculaneum beckoned, affording a look into the life of humans who trod these streets millennia ago. Standing among the preserved artifacts of a bygone period, I was overwhelmed by the weight of history that surrounded me.

No vacation to Naples would be complete without sampling its gastronomic pleasures. From delectable pizzas topped with locally produced ingredients to indulgent platters of spaghetti alle vongole, each meal celebrated the region's culinary skill.

Beyond its architectural grandeur and culinary pleasures, the friendliness and generosity of the Neapolitan people made the most effect on me. Whether I was telling tales with a local barista over a frothy cappuccino or getting lost in discussion with other travelers at a crowded trattoria, I felt at home in this dynamic city.

About Napoli

Napoli, sometimes known as Naples in English, is a dynamic and historically significant city in southern Italy. Nestled in the scenic Bay of Naples, with the majestic Mount Vesuvius nearby, the city has a rich cultural legacy, magnificent architecture, and delectable food. Napoli, founded by the Greeks in the eighth century BC, has long been an important city in the Mediterranean, functioning as a major cultural and commercial center. Its strategic position made it a crossroads for trade, business, and cultural interaction, resulting in a distinct combination of influences from numerous civilizations. The Castel Nuovo, a medieval castle, is one of Napoli's most famous buildings, representing the city's rich history and architectural splendor. The old center of Naples, a UNESCO World Heritage Site, is a maze of small cobblestone alleys surrounded with colorful houses, vibrant piazzas, and elegant churches. Piazza del Plebiscito, with its imposing Royal Palace and San Francesco di Paola cathedral, is a symbol of the city's grandeur.

Napoli is well-known for its gastronomic pleasures, and Neapolitan food is popular internationally. The city's culinary choices range from classic pizzas made in wood-fired ovens to savory pasta dishes like spaghetti alle vongole (spaghetti with clams) and robust ragù alla napoletana (Neapolitan-style meat sauce). Visitors may eat delicious street cuisine like arancini (rice balls) and sfogliatella (shell-shaped pastries), or have a leisurely lunch at one of the city's trattorias or posh restaurants.

The city's cultural sector is likewise thriving, with various museums, theaters, and art galleries displaying Napoli's rich creative legacy. The National Archaeological Museum has an extraordinary collection of artifacts from Pompeii and Herculaneum, which provide insights into ancient Roman everyday life. The Teatro di San Carlo, one of the world's oldest opera theaters, continues to captivate spectators with its breathtaking performances.

Despite its ancient appeal, Napoli is a city that values modernism and innovation. The busy port serves as a gateway to the Mediterranean, and the city's universities and research organizations help to improve science, technology, and academics.

However, Napoli confronts a number of obstacles, including economic disparities, organized crime, and infrastructural concerns. Despite these hurdles, the Neapolitan people's perseverance and spirit come through as they struggle to preserve their cultural legacy and create a better future for their beloved city.

Why Napoli Is a Must-Visit Destination

There are several reasons why Naples, often known as Napoli, is an enthralling location. As shown by the archeological sites that it contains, like Pompeii and Herculaneum, its long and illustrious history extends back to ancient times. A large number of tourists are unable to resist the city's dynamic culture, which is reflected in its food, music, and art. In addition, Naples is home to incredible architectural masterpieces, such as magnificent palaces and cathedrals. In addition to its attraction, the fact that it is located in close proximity to the scenic Amalfi Coast and the island of Capri makes it an essential destination for tourists who are interested in history, culture, and natural beauty.

CHAPTER 1: PLANNING YOUR TRIP TO NAPOLI

Planning a vacation to Naples may be both exhilarating and daunting. Choosing where to begin might be challenging due to the abundance of sights and activities available. With little planning and study, you can plan a schedule to maximize your time in this great city.

This chapter will walk you through the planning process, including picking when to travel and selecting the best hotels and transportation alternatives. I will provide recommendations for navigating the city, including transportation, dining options, and packing essentials.

This chapter will help you organize a wonderful vacation to Napoli based on your interests, budget, and travel style, whether you are a first-time visitor or a seasoned traveler. Let's start organizing your vacation to one of the world's most intriguing places.

When to Visit Napoli

Naples, or Napoli, is a dynamic city in southern Italy famed for its rich history, gorgeous architecture, wonderful food, and the kindness of its people. Choosing the ideal time to visit Napoli mostly relies on your choices for weather, people, and events. Here's an overview of the various seasons to help you determine when to schedule your trip:

Spring (March to May):
Spring is a lovely season to visit Napoli since the weather is moderate and pleasant. Temperatures vary from roughly 10°C (50°F) to 20°C (68°F), making it suitable for exploring the city on foot.
This season sees less people compared to the busy summer months, so you can experience iconic destinations like Pompeii, Mount Vesuvius, and the Amalfi Coast without fighting enormous crowds.
Spring also brings bright blossoms to the city's parks and gardens, adding to its appeal.

Summer (June to August):
Summer is the peak tourist season in Napoli, with mild temperatures ranging from 25°C (77°F) and 30°C (86°F). It's excellent for sun-seekers who wish to enjoy the city's beaches and outdoor cafés.

However, be prepared for more crowds and higher pricing during this period. Popular tourist attractions may grow crowded, and lodgings may be more costly.Despite the crowds, summer is also when Napoli comes alive with festivals, concerts, and cultural activities. The city's streets hum with activity, giving a bustling environment for tourists.

Autumn (September to November):
Autumn is another fantastic season to visit Napoli, since the weather stays comfortable, and visitor crowds tend to decrease down after the summer peak. Temperatures gradually fall down, ranging from roughly 20°C (68°F) to 10°C (50°F), making it pleasant for touring and seeing the city's highlights. Autumn also marks the harvest season, allowing opportunity to experience fresh local food and enjoy classic Italian cuisine at its best.

Winter (December to February):
Winter in Napoli is moderate compared to northern Europe, with temperatures averaging between 5°C (41°F) and 15°C (59°F). While it may not be beach weather, it's still a fantastic time to come if you want fewer people and reduced pricing. The city's festive ambiance throughout the holiday season, featuring Christmas markets and decorations, gives a distinct appeal to Napoli in winter.

However, certain sites and restaurants may have restricted hours or be closed during the offseason, so it's crucial to verify in advance. Ultimately, the greatest time to visit Napoli depends on your interests and what experiences you're seeking. Whether you're attracted to the bustling summer atmosphere, the pleasant weather of spring and fall, or the calmer ambiance of winter, Napoli provides something for every traveler year-round.

How to Get to Napoli

Napoli, Italy, is a significant transportation center in southern Italy, thus getting there is rather straightforward. Here are a few methods to go to Naples:

By Air:
Naples International Airport (Aeroporto di Napoli-Capodichino) is situated around 7 km northeast of the city center. It accepts both local and foreign flights. You may take a cab, an airport shuttle, or the Alibus, a specialized shuttle service that runs from the airport to the city center and the major train station (Napoli Centrale).

By Train:
Napoli Centrale is the city's primary rail station, with connections to important cities around Italy and Europe. High-speed trains (Frecciarossa and Italo) travel regularly between Naples and cities such as Rome, Florence, Milan, and Venice. The

Circumvesuviana railway links Napoli to adjacent destinations including Pompeii, Sorrento, and the Amalfi Coast. Trains depart from Napoli Centrale and Napoli Porta Nolana stations.

By Bus:
Napoli is serviced by a number of long-distance bus operators, notably FlixBus and MarinoBus, which link the city to numerous locations around Italy and Europe.The major bus terminal in Napoli is situated close to the Napoli Centrale train station, making it easy for bus passengers to reach the city center.

By Car:
Napoli is easily accessible by vehicle because of Italy's large highway network. The A1 Autostrada del Sole connects Napoli and Rome, while the A3 Autostrada Napoli-Salerno connects the city to the Amalfi Coast and southern Italy. Keep in mind that driving in Naples might be difficult owing to traffic congestion and restricted parking, particularly in the old city center. Consider leaving your vehicle outside the city center and exploring Napoli by public transit.

By Ferry:
Napoli is a large port city with ferry links to a variety of Italian and international locations. Ferries go between Napoli and the islands of Capri, Ischia, and Procida, as well as ports in Sicily, Sardinia, and other Mediterranean nations. Regardless of how you choose to travel, Napoli's central position and many transit choices make it easy to reach from inside Italy and beyond, assuring a seamless trip to this interesting city.

Getting Around Napoli

With a vast public transit system and plenty of walking and cycling routes, getting about Napoli, Italy, is comparatively simple. The following are the primary means of travel in Naples:

Metro: Piscinala, Garibaldi, Vanvitelli, Pozzuoli, Garibaldi, Gianturco, and Line 6 (Mergellina, Mostra, Augusteo) make up Napoli's metro system.

The city's major sights, including Piazza del Plebiscito, Castel Nuovo, and the Archaeological Museum, may be easily reached by metro, which operates with efficiency and convenience.

Bus:
AMT (Azienda Mobilità e Trasporti) runs a vast bus network in Napoli that serves the city's perimeter as well as the city center. Bus lines are a viable way to go to places that aren't covered by the metro or tram since they travel almost all across the city.

Tram:
There are three lines in the Napoli tram system: Line 1 (Piazza Garibaldi - Poggioreale - Stazione Marittima), Line 4 (Augusteo - Piazza Carlo III - Arzano), and Line 6 (Piazza Municipio - Piazza Garibaldi - Arzano). Line 1, which provides views of Mount Vesuvius and the Gulf of Napoli, is a particularly picturesque district of Napoli to explore by tram.

In Napoli, there are four funicular railroads that link various regions of the city, such as Chiaia, Montesanto, Mergellina, and Central Station. Funiculars provide sweeping views of the city and the Bay of Napoli in addition to being a useful means of transportation.

Taxi:
Taxis may be reserved in advance or hailed on the street, and they are easily found around Napoli. Taxis are a practical way to go short distances or to

locations that are difficult to get by public transit. The old city center of Napoli is a great place to explore on foot since it has a lot of the city's attractions.

Walking:
You may take your time exploring Napoli's lively piazzas, historical sites, and colorful streets by walking.

Cycling:
Napoli is progressively becoming more bike-friendly, with certain sections having bike-sharing programmes and bike lanes. Especially in parks like Villa Comunale or along the seaside, cycling may be a fun way to discover Napoli.

Napoli offers a variety of transit alternatives to meet your requirements and interests, making it simple and economical to go about.

Choosing the Right Accommodation

Choosing the proper hotels in Napoli, Italy, is vital for ensuring a comfortable and pleasurable stay in this dynamic city. Here are some aspects to consider while picking where to stay:

Location:
Determine the areas of Napoli you want to visit most often and select lodgings that are centrally placed or well-connected to public transportation. The historic city center (Centro Storico) is a popular option for its accessibility to key sights, restaurants, and retail districts. Other areas like Chiaia, Vomero, and Posillipo provide a more upmarket ambiance with spectacular views of the Bay of Napoli. If you're coming by rail, lodgings near Napoli Centrale train station might be ideal for quick access to public transit.

Budget:
Establish a budget for your lodgings and examine possibilities that are within your pricing range. Napoli provides a broad selection of lodgings, including luxury hotels, boutique hotels, budget hotels, bed & breakfasts, hostels, and vacation rentals. Keep in mind that costs may vary based on the season, location, and facilities supplied by the property.

Amenities:
Consider the amenities and facilities given by the hotels, such as free Wi-Fi, air conditioning, breakfast, 24-hour reception, parking, and laundry services. If you value particular facilities, such as a

gym, spa, or rooftop terrace with panoramic views, favor lodgings that provide these advantages.

Reviews and Ratings:
Read reviews and ratings from past guests to judge the quality and dependability of the lodgings.

Websites like TripAdvisor, Booking.com, and Airbnb give useful information from genuine tourists about their experiences staying at different lodgings in Napoli.

Safety and Security:
Prioritize hotels in safe and secure districts, especially if you want to explore the city on foot or return late at night. Look for lodgings with secure entry, such as key cards or 24-hour reception, to safeguard the safety of yourself and your things.

Local Charm:
Consider staying in places that represent the local culture and charm of Napoli, such as classic boutique hotels, traditional bed & breakfasts, or quaint guesthouses. Staying in lodgings with distinct character and individuality may improve your entire experience and absorption in the city's culture.

Flexibility:
Remain flexible with your lodgings, particularly during peak tourist seasons when availability may be restricted or rates higher. Consider reserving lodgings with flexible cancellation policies in case your vacation plans alter suddenly.

By considering these elements and completing comprehensive research, you can find the perfect lodgings in Napoli that match your requirements, tastes, and budget, assuring a memorable and pleasurable stay in this interesting city.

What to Pack

When preparing for a vacation to Napoli, Italy, keep the Mediterranean temperature, variety of activities, and cultural standards in mind. Here's a thorough packing list to help you prepare for your visit:

Clothes:
Bring lightweight, breathable clothes for warm weather, such as shorts, t-shirts, and sundresses.

For chilly nights, wear light layers, such as a jumper or jacket. Bring comfortable walking shoes for exploring the city's cobblestone streets and mountainous landscape.

Swimsuit and beachwear if you intend on visiting neighboring beaches or coastal regions. Use a hat, sunglasses, and sunscreen to protect yourself from the sun's rays.

Accessories:
Crossbody bag or backpack for transporting necessities while sightseeing. Bring an umbrella or rain jacket, particularly if coming in the spring or fall, when rains are more common. If you are traveling from outside Europe, you will need electrical adapters and converters for European outlets. A portable power bank for charging your electronics while you're on the road.

Documents and Money:
Passport, visa (if applicable), and travel insurance. Transactions must be made using euros or international credit/debit cards. Hotel bookings, airplane tickets, and itineraries, either printed or digital.

Personal Items:
Toiletries, such as shampoo, conditioner, soap, toothbrush, and any necessary prescriptions. A basic first-aid package that includes bandages, pain relievers, and any prescribed drugs. Hand sanitizer

and disinfection wipes in travel size to keep you clean while traveling.

Electronics:
Smartphone and charger for navigation, communication, and memory capture. A camera or GoPro to chronicle your activities and capture the beauty of Naples. Bring a lightweight portable laptop or tablet if you need to keep connected or work remotely. Headphones or earbuds to listen to music, podcasts, or audio guides while touring.

Guidebooks and Maps:
Use guides or travel apps to organize your schedule and explore Napoli's attractions. Use city maps or offline navigation applications to navigate the streets and neighborhoods of Naples.

Cultural Considerations:
Dress modestly while visiting religious places such as churches and cathedrals. If necessary, use a scarf or shawl to cover your shoulders and knees while entering sacred institutions.

Appropriate apparel for eating out or visiting cultural activities, such as sophisticated casual evening wear.

Optional Extras:
Travel diary or notepad for capturing memories and experiences. Snacks and a reusable water bottle to keep you hydrated and fuelled on your excursion.
To carry souvenirs or groceries, use a foldable tote bag or reusable shopping bag.

You may assure a comfortable and joyful exploration of this wonderful city by packing intelligently and taking into account your unique requirements.

Visa and Entry Requirements

As of 2024, the visa and entrance procedures for going to Napoli, Italy, are substantially identical with prior years. Here's a thorough resource to help you understand the visa and entrance requirements for your trip:

Schengen Visa:
Italy is a part of the Schengen Area, enabling people of specified countries to enter Italy and other Schengen nations for short periods (up to 90 days (within a 180 day term) without a visa. Citizens of Schengen Area nations, as well as numerous additional countries including the United States, Canada, Australia, and Japan, normally do not

require a visa for short trips for tourists, work, or visiting friends and family.

Visa-Free Travel:
Citizens of Schengen Area nations and select other countries may enter Italy and remain for up to 90 days during a 180 day period without a visa. It's vital to verify whether your country is among those excluded from the Schengen Visa requirement or whether you qualify for visa free travel before arranging your trip to Napoli.

Visa Requirements:
If you are a citizen of a nation that is not visa exempt for short visits in the Schengen Area, you will need to apply for a Schengen Visa (Type C visa) from the Italian consulate or embassy in your home country before going. Schengen Visa applications normally involve paperwork such as a valid passport, evidence of travel plans, travel insurance, proof of lodging, financial means to fund your stay, and a completed visa application form.

Long Term remain and Work Visas:
If you want to remain in Italy for more than 90 days or intend to work, study, or participate in other long term activities, you may need to apply for a

different form of visa, such as a National Visa (form D visa) or a particular residence or work permit.

Long term visa requirements and application procedures may be more difficult and may need extra paperwork, such as a letter of admission from an Italian institution (for students) or a job offer letter (for workers).

Entry Requirements:
All passengers entering Italy must have a valid passport with at least six months' validity beyond the anticipated term of stay. Border officials may also ask for evidence of adequate finances to support your stay and return or further travel plans. Upon admission, you may be subject to passport inspection and interrogation by immigration authorities. Therefore, it's vital to have all appropriate paperwork and information readily accessible.

Before planning your trip to Napoli, it's vital to verify the most up to date visa and entrance requirements for your country since restrictions might differ and may be subject to change. You may visit the website of the Italian Ministry of Foreign Affairs or call the closest Italian consulate or embassy for the latest information and help on visa applications and entrance requirements.

Currency and Language

Napoli, Italy is part of the Campania region and shares the same currency and language as the rest of Italy:

Currency:
The Euro (€) is the official currency of Napoli and Italy as a whole.

Euros are represented by banknotes (€5, €10, €20, €50, €100, €200, and €500) and coins (1 cent, 2 cents, 5 cents, 10 cents, 20 cents, 50 cents, €1, and €2). Currency exchange services are widely accessible at Napoli's airports, banks, exchange offices, and certain hotels. Furthermore, ATMs are widely available and accept major international credit and debit cards for withdrawing euros.

Language:
Italian is the major language spoken in Naples and across Italy. Some inhabitants, notably the older generation, speak Neapolitan, a unique regional dialect with origins in Latin. However, Italian is the most often used language in official situations, commercial transactions, and daily contact. English

is widely spoken and understood in tourist areas, hotels, restaurants, especially among younger generations in Naples.

However, it is usually recommended to learn a few simple Italian words or pleasantries to improve your relationships with people and demonstrate respect for their culture.

Suggested Budget

Creating a proposed budget for a trip to Napoli relies on numerous elements, including your travel style, interests, and the length of your stay. Here's a list of likely expenditures to consider while organizing your budget for Napoli:

Accommodation:
Accommodation fees in Napoli vary based on the sort of accommodation you pick, ranging from cheap hostels and guesthouses to luxury hotels and vacation homes.

On average, budget tourists may expect to pay roughly €40-€80 per night for a hostel or budget hotel, while mid-range lodgings may vary from €80-€150 per night. Luxury hotels and boutique lodgings may surpass €150 per night. Consider your preferred degree of comfort and facilities while spending for lodging in Napoli.

Food and Dining:
Napoli is famed for its superb cuisine, including pizza, spaghetti, seafood, and pastries. Dining out may be a considerable investment, but there are solutions to fit every budget.

A budget visitor might anticipate to pay roughly €10-€20 for a simple dinner at a pizza, trattoria, or street food stand. Mid-range restaurants may charge €20-€40 per person for a three-course dinner, whereas upmarket dining facilities might reach €50 per person.

Additionally, pay for snacks, beverages, and groceries if you want to self-cater or enjoy picnics in Napoli's parks or along the seaside.

Transportation:
Public transportation in Napoli, including buses, metro, trams, and funiculars, is inexpensive and efficient. A single metro or bus ticket normally costs roughly €1.50, whereas day passes or multi-day tickets provide discounts for regular users.

Consider obtaining a Napoli Card, which allows unlimited access to public transit and discounts on museums and attractions. If you wish to travel beyond Napoli, pay for transportation to neighboring attractions such as Pompeii, Sorrento, or the Amalfi Coast, which may need extra train, bus, or boat tickets.

Attractions and Activities:
Napoli provides a multitude of attractions, museums, and cultural experiences to enjoy. Budget for entry fees to major places such as Castel Nuovo, the Archaeological Museum, and the Catacombs of San Gennaro. Guided tours, boat rides, and excursions to neighboring locations like Pompeii or Mount Vesuvius may impose extra charges.

Consider getting a city pass or combo ticket to save money on admission costs to several sites.

Miscellaneous Expenditures:
Budget for miscellaneous expenditures such as souvenirs, shopping, washing, and unplanned charges. Tipping is not necessary in Italy, although it's traditional to round up the bill or offer a little tip for exceptional service, especially in restaurants.

Overall, a recommended daily budget for a visitor visiting Napoli might vary from €50 to €150 or more, depending on your interests and spending patterns. By planning and spending correctly, you may have a great and cheap vacation to this intriguing city in southern Italy.

Money-Saving Tips

Traveling to Naples may be fun and inexpensive . Here are some money-saving strategies to help you get the most out of your vacation while keeping within your budget:

Travel Off-Season:
Visit Napoli during the shoulder seasons of spring (March-May) or autumn (September-November) for reduced hotel costs and less crowded tourist sites.

Avoid traveling during busy tourist seasons, such as summer (June to August), when accommodations and activities are often more expensive.

Book Accommodation in Advance:
Secure reduced prices by researching and booking ahead of time. If you're traveling on a limited budget, look for affordable choices like hostels, guesthouses, or vacation rentals.

Use Public Transit:
Take use of Napoli's economical and efficient public transit network, which includes buses, metro, trams, and funiculars to travel about the city.

Consider buying day passes or multi-day tickets for unrestricted travel, which are cheaper than purchasing individual tickets for each excursion.

Eat Like a Local:
Enjoy traditional Neapolitan cuisine at local pizzerias, trattorias, and street food vendors, which are typically more affordable than tourist establishments.

Look for daily specials, set menus, or "pranzo" (lunch) discounts at restaurants to get the most value for your money.

Pack Picnics and Snacks:
Avoid eating out by bringing your own food. Fresh vegetables, bread, cheese, and other picnic staples may be purchased at local markets or supermarkets. While taking in the ambiance of Napoli, have a picnic at one of the city's gorgeous parks or stunning vistas.

Take Advantage of Free Activities:
Visit Napoli's free attractions, including Piazza del Plebiscito, the ancient city center, and lively street markets. Attend free events, festivals, or cultural performances held across the city, which provide possibilities for cultural immersion without cost.

Visit Museums on Free Entrance Days:
Some museums and cultural attractions in Napoli provide free entrance on specified dates or hours. Plan your vacation to take advantage of these free entry days and enjoy Napoli's rich history and cultural heritage without having to pay entrance fees.

Stay Hydrated with Tap Water:
Avoid buying bottled water by refilling reusable bottles with safe tap water in Napoli and around Italy. Bring a refillable water bottle to remain hydrated while visiting and enjoying the city.

Shop Smart for Souvenirs:
Avoid tourist traps and high costs by buying souvenirs from local markets, artisan workshops, or independent stores. Look for one-of-a-kind and genuine souvenirs, such as handmade pottery, local delicacies, or artisanal items, that will make

memorable presents and memories of your vacation to Naples.

By following these money saving strategies, you may have an inexpensive and memorable vacation in Napoli without sacrificing quality or fun. Best wishes for your trip!

Best Places to Book Your Trip

When arranging your trip to Napoli, be sure to choose trustworthy platforms or travel companies to guarantee a seamless and comfortable experience. Here are some of the finest sites to plan your vacation to Naples:

Online Travel Agencies (OTAs):
Booking.com, Expedia, and TripAdvisor provide many lodging alternatives in Napoli, such as hotels, hostels, guesthouses, and vacation rentals. These services enable you to compare pricing, read prior guests' reviews, and book rooms straight online.

Some OTAs also offer package offers that include flights, lodgings, and other services, which provide travelers with convenience and the opportunity for savings.

Airline Websites:
When buying tickets to Naples, visit the websites of major airlines that fly to Naples International Airport (NAP). Airlines such as Alitalia, Ryanair, easyJet, and Lufthansa provide direct flights to Napoli from locations around Europe and beyond.

Booking directly via airline websites may sometimes result in unique bargains, promotions, or loyalty points for frequent fliers.

Hotel and Accommodation Websites:
Many Napoli hotels and accommodations provide direct booking via their websites. Booking directly via the hotel's website may occasionally result in benefits such as lower prices, free upgrades, or more flexible cancellation policies.

It's recommended calling hotels directly to check about special deals or discounts if you book via them.

Holiday Rental Platforms:
Airbnb, Vrbo, and HomeAway provide a diverse range of holiday rentals in Napoli, such as apartments, villas, and homes. These sites enable you to explore listings, contact with hosts, and book lodgings based on your interests and budget.

Vacation rentals might be a fantastic choice for travelers who want more room, privacy, and flexibility during their stay in Napoli.

Travel Agencies and Tour Operators:
For more personalized trip planning, book with a respected agency or tour operator.

Travel firms can help you plan customized itineraries, guided tours, transportation, and other services based on your choices and interests.
Look for firms who specialize in Italy, particularly Napoli, since they may have insider information and local contacts that may improve your trip.

Package Holidays:
Tour operators and travel companies provide simple and hassle-free choices for planning your vacation to Napoli. - Package vacations often include flights, lodgings, and, on occasion, extra services such as airport transfers, excursions, or activities.

Look for package offers that are suited to your specific needs, whether you want a cultural city break, a beach trip, or a gourmet excursion in Napoli.

Regardless of where you book your Napoli vacation, be sure to do full research, read reviews, and compare rates to discover the greatest bargains and alternatives that meet your travel requirements and tastes. Booking in advance may also assist to ensure availability and perhaps save money on flights and lodging.

CHAPTER 2: GETTING TO KNOW NAPOLI

Getting to know Napoli is an amazing experience. Start with a visit to its old center, a UNESCO World Heritage Site, where you can explore tiny alleys lined with colorful architecture, busy marketplaces, and vivid piazzas. Don't miss the prominent monuments like Castel Nuovo and the Royal Palace of Naples.

Indulge in Napoli's gastronomic pleasures by savoring traditional Neapolitan pizza, sfogliatella pastries, and fresh seafood at local trattorias and pizzerias. Dive into the city's rich history at the National Archaeological Museum, home to treasures from Pompeii, Herculaneum, and ancient Greece.

Take a walk along the waterfront promenade, Lungomare, for panoramic views of the Bay of Naples and Mount Vesuvius. And for a day excursion, discover the neighboring sites such as the ruins of Pompeii, the magnificent Amalfi Coast, or the quaint island of Capri.

Immerse yourself in Napoli's bustling environment, where the enthusiasm for life, art, and cuisine is obvious at every step.

A Brief History of Napoli

Napoli, one of Italy's oldest continuously inhabited cities, with a history spanning over 2,800 years. Founded as Neápolis by Greek immigrants in the 8th century BC, it grew to become a prominent cultural and economic hub under numerous rulers, including the Greeks, Romans, Byzantines, Normans, Angevins, and Aragonese.

Napoli thrived as a key port city throughout the Roman Empire, and the well-preserved remains of Pompeii and Herculaneum, which were buried by Mount Vesuvius' eruption in 79 AD, provide proof of its historic history.

In the Middle Ages, Napoli became the capital of the Kingdom of Naples, which was controlled by several dynasties such as the Angevins, Aragonese, and Bourbon kings. The city had periods of wealth, artistic blossoming, as well as political upheaval and foreign invasions.

Napoli was one of Europe's greatest and most affluent towns in the 18th century, with a reputation for Baroque architecture, music, and art. However, it also faced problems, such as illness outbreaks and societal unrest.

Napoli was a key player in Italy's unification, known as the Risorgimento, and joined the Kingdom of Italy in 1861.

Throughout the twentieth century, Napoli saw fast urbanization and economic progress, as well as social challenges including organized crime and political corruption.

Today, Napoli is a thriving cultural city that combines old history with contemporary living, and it continues to amaze tourists with its rich past, gastronomic pleasures, and breathtaking scenery.

Understanding the History of Napoli

Understanding Napoli's culture entails digging into its unique fabric of customs, art, food, and social dynamics. Here's a look at what makes Napoli's culture distinctive:

Passion and Vibrancy:
Napoli is renowned for its passionate and dynamic environment. The city pulsates with vitality, whether it's via loud street discussions, emotional gestures by its citizens, or fanatical love for its football club, SSC Napoli.

Cuisine:
Neapolitan cuisine is world-renowned for its simplicity and deliciousness. From the renowned Neapolitan pizza made with San Marzano tomatoes and buffalo mozzarella to pasta dishes like spaghetti alle vongole (spaghetti with clams), Napoli's culinary culture reflects the city's rich history and closeness to the sea.

Music and Arts:
Napoli has a rich musical and artistic legacy. The city is famed for its Neapolitan songs, which often express themes of love, desire, and regret. Furthermore, Napoli has a lively modern art scene, with galleries and street art contributing to its cultural environment.

Religion and Festivals:
Religion is important in Napoli culture, with Catholicism being the most popular religion. Throughout the year, the city celebrates several

religious festivals and processions, notably the Feast of San Gennaro, Napoli's patron saint, which is widely celebrated.

Street Life and Socializing:
Napoli's streets serve as social centers, with inhabitants gathering to mingle, play cards, and sip espresso at one of the numerous cafes. Piazzas like Piazza del Plebiscito and Piazza Dante are alive with activity, providing a look into the city's social character.

Resilience and Pride:
Despite experiencing problems including economic hardship and organized crime, Napoli inhabitants have a strong feeling of resilience and pride in their hometown and history. This fortitude is evident in their strong feeling of community and resolve to protect Napoli's historic heritage.

Understanding Napoli's culture entails not just examining its superficial components, but also recognizing the passion, history, and complexity that shape the city's character.

CHAPTER 3: EXPLORING NAPOLI'S NEIGHBORHOODS

Napoli is a city that provides a myriad of distinctive and distinct neighborhoods that are excellent for tourists to discover. Each neighborhood has its own individuality, giving something different and intriguing to discover.

In this chapter, I'll lead you through some of the most popular neighborhoods in Napoli. Here's an overview of some of Napoli's most noteworthy neighborhoods. We'll start by touring the busy retail area of Centro Storico famed for its historic architecture, traditional Neapolitan food, cultural legacy and active street life of Spaccanapoli. Then, we'll have a tour around Chiaia, Vomero, Posillipo, Spanish Quarter, Sanita. Each district has its own individual character, attractions and experiences, adding to the rich fabric of Napoli.

Centro Storico

Napoli's Centro Storico, or Historic Center, is a vibrant and interesting area that serves as the heart of the city. This UNESCO World Heritage Site is a maze of narrow streets, ancient churches, and grand piazzas that give visitors a glimpse into

Napoli's rich and interesting past. Here's an overview of what to expect in this historic area.

Piazza del Plebiscito:
The Centro Storico is centered around Piazza del Plebiscito, one of Napoli's most important squares and a symbol of the city's grandeur. The Piazza, which is bordered by the Royal Palace of Naples and the Basilica of San Francesco di Paola, is an architectural masterpiece and a popular gathering place for both locals and tourists.

Spaccanapoli:
Spaccanapoli, often known as the "Naples Splitter," is a long, straight street that splits Naples' historic city in two. Spaccanapoli, which is surrounded with shops, cafés, and centuries-old buildings, is great for experiencing Napoli's hectic character.

San Gregorio Armeno:
This small street is famed for its artisan workshops and businesses that sell presepi, or nativity scenes. Visitors may wander along this picturesque street, enjoying the exquisite handmade sculptures and decorations that are a common Napoli tradition.

Castel Nuovo (Maschio Angioino):
Castel Nuovo, also known as Maschio Angioino, is a Medieval fortification erected near the seaside. The castle, erected in the 13th century, is an iconic landmark in Napoli, offering panoramic views of the city and port from its battlements.

The Napoli Underground:
Napoli Sotterranea, often known as the Napoli Underground, is a hidden world of tunnels, tombs, and ancient ruins under the Centro Storico's streets. Visitors may take guided tours of this fascinating subterranean world, learning about Napoli's history and the secrets concealed under its streets.

Chiesa del Gesù Nuovo:
The lovely Baroque church is located in Piazza del Gesù Nuovo. Its front is ornamented with intricate brickwork and artistic embellishments, while the inside is filled with breathtaking paintings and sculptures.

National Archaeological Museum of Naples:
The National Archaeological Museum of Naples has one of the world's most extensive collections of Greek and Roman relics. Visitors may see the

ancient sculptures, mosaics, and wealth uncovered in Pompeii and Herculaneum.

Street Dining:
The Centro Storico is a foodie's paradise, with several trattorias, pizzerias, and street food vendors providing delectable Neapolitan fare. Don't miss the chance to eat authentic Margherita pizza, fried street snacks like arancini and sfogliatelle, and other regional favorites.

Napoli's Centro Storico is a vibrant and dynamic district that invites visitors to wander its winding streets, uncover hidden jewels, and immerse themselves in the city's rich tapestry of history and culture. Whether you're admiring historic buildings, sampling street food, or just soaking in the atmosphere in a vibrant area, the Centro Storico offers a one of a kind experience in the heart of Naples.

Chiaia

Chiaia is a fashionable and wealthy neighborhood set along Naples' scenic shoreline, providing a mix of elegance, charm, and Mediterranean beauty. Chiaia, located in the center of Napoli, is known for its expensive stores, bustling cultural scene, and breathtaking views of the Bay of Naples. Here's what to anticipate while touring Chiaia:

Via Chiaia:
Via Chiaia is the neighborhood's major road, a lively boulevard dotted with beautiful boutiques, luxury shops, and trendy cafés. It's ideal for a leisurely walk or some luxury shopping, with a mix of foreign companies and local craftsmen displaying their items.

Piazza dei Martiri:
Piazza dei Martiri, or Martyrs' area, is a lovely area in the middle of Chiaia, surrounded by old houses, cafés, and restaurants. It is a favorite gathering place for both residents and tourists, providing a tranquil respite from the hectic streets around.

Villa Comunale:
Villa Comunale is a lovely park that runs along the Naples coastline, with lush foliage, groomed gardens, and breathtaking views of the Bay of Naples and Mount Vesuvius. It's ideal for a relaxing walk, a picnic with friends, or a romantic sunset walk.

Palazzo delle Arti Napoli (PAN):
The Palazzo delle Arti Napoli (PAN) is a cultural center located in a medieval palace in Chiaia. Throughout the year, it holds art exhibits, concerts, plays, and other cultural events that highlight Napoli's greatest modern and traditional art.

Seafront Promenade:
Chiaia has a magnificent coastal promenade where both inhabitants and tourists may enjoy the invigorating sea wind, soak up the sun, and take in the breathtaking views of the Bay of Napoli. It's a popular place to go running, cycling, or just rest by the river.

Cultural Attractions:
Chiaia has various cultural attractions, including the Museum of Villa Pignatelli and the Castel dell'Ovo, a medieval fortification built on a rocky islet at the entrance to the Naples harbor. Visitors may tour these historic sites and learn about the neighborhood's rich history.

Dinner and Nightlife:
Chiaia has a diversified culinary scene, with a variety of restaurants, cafés, and taverns providing anything from traditional Neapolitan cuisine to foreign dishes. Whether you're hungry for seafood,

pizza, or gourmet cuisine, Chiaia has lots of alternatives to suit your taste.

Chiaia's combination of refinement, culture, and natural beauty makes it a must-see location in Naples. Whether you're strolling through its quaint streets, resting in its lush parks, or enjoying its thriving cultural scene, Chiaia provides a remarkable experience that reflects the spirit of Napoli's seaside appeal.

Vomero

Vomero is a charming and wealthy neighborhood perched atop a hill facing the city of Napoli, offering amazing panoramic views of the Bay of Naples and Mount Vesuvius. Known for its beautiful buildings, tree-lined streets, and cultural draws, Vomero is a famous living and tourist spot in Napoli. Here's a better look at what Vomero has to offer:

Castel Sant'Elmo:
One of Vomero's most famous features is Castel Sant'Elmo, an ancient fortress that dominates the skyline of Napoli. Built in the 14th century, the castle offers stunning views of the city and the bay from its strategic high site. Visitors can experience

the castle's walls, gardens, and exhibits, learning about its interesting past and importance.
Certosa di San Martino:

Adjacent to Castel Sant'Elmo is the Certosa di San Martino, a former convent and now a museum complex. This Baroque marvel houses a rich collection of art, artifacts, and holy treasures, as well as beautifully kept cloisters, churches, and gardens. The Certosa di San Martino offers a look into the spiritual and cultural history of Napoli.
Viale Michelangelo:

Viale Michelangelo is Vomero's main road, a tree-lined boulevard surrounded by elegant buildings, cafes, and shops. It's the perfect place for a relaxed walk or a spot of shopping, with plenty of chances to enjoy the neighborhood's polished atmosphere and building beauty.
Villa Floridiana:

Villa Floridiana is a beautiful park found in the heart of Vomero, giving a peaceful oasis amid the busy city. Visitors can walk through its planted grounds, admire its neoclassical house, and enjoy sweeping views of Napoli and the bay. The park is a favorite spot for picnics, relaxing walks, and outdoor relaxation.

Shopping and Dining:
Vomero boasts a lively food scene, with a wide range of restaurants, cafes, and trattorias serving delicious Neapolitan cuisine and foreign fare. From traditional pizzerias to fancy eating places, there's something to fit every taste in Vomero.

The area also offers excellent buying options, with chic shops, brand stores, and craft businesses lining its streets. Whether you're looking for clothes, home decor, or gifts, you'll find plenty of choices to explore in Vomero.

Cultural Events and Festivals:
Throughout the year, Vomero hosts a variety of cultural events, festivals, and shows celebrating art, music, and history. From outdoor concerts and street markets to art projects and theater shows, there's always something going on in Vomero to delight locals and tourists alike.

Vomero's mix of natural beauty, cultural history, and stylish charm makes it a must-visit location in Napoli. Whether you're discovering its historic landmarks, indulging in its culinary delights, or simply enjoying its sweeping views, Vomero offers a unique experience that captures the spirit of Napoli's timeless charm.

Posillipo

Posillipo is a lovely and private neighborhood set along Napoli's craggy coastline, known for its spectacular views of the Bay of Naples, luxury houses, and calm atmosphere. Posillipo, located on the city's western side, emits an atmosphere of elegance and natural beauty that has long drawn nobles, artists, and discriminating travelers looking for a calm vacation. Here's what to anticipate while touring Posillipo:

Gorgeous Coastal Drive:
Posillipo is known for its gorgeous coastal route, Via Posillipo, which runs along the steep cliffs overlooking the Bay of Napoli. The journey provides panoramic views of the turquoise seas below, the distant silhouette of Mount Vesuvius, and the picturesque fishing towns that dot the coastline.

Villas and Palaces:
Posillipo is peppered with opulent mansions, palaces, and ancient houses that reflect the area's rich legacy and prominent past. These beautiful mansions, many of which date back to the 19th century, are surrounded by lush gardens, terraces, and private beaches, providing an insight into the lavish lifestyle of Naples' elite.

Parco Virgiliano:

Located on Posillipo hill, Parco Virgiliano provides magnificent views of the Bay of Napoli and the surrounding coastline. Visitors may stroll around its beautiful gardens, rest in shady woodlands, or have a leisurely picnic while admiring the breathtaking views below.

Gaiola Underwater Park:

Gaiola Underwater Park is a protected marine region off the coast of Posillipo known for its crystal-clear seas, abundant marine life, and underwater ancient artifacts. Visitors may enjoy the park's clean beaches, swim or dive, or take a boat excursion to see the underwater remnants of old villas and Roman fish farms.

Marechiaro Beach:

This quiet beach at the foot of the Posillipo cliffs provides a peaceful respite from the city. The beach is recognised for its crystal-clear waters, rocky outcrops, and spectacular environment, making it a popular swimming, sunbathing, and leisure destination.

Seafood Restaurants:

Posillipo has some of Napoli's top seafood restaurants, providing fresh catches of the day in a scenic beachfront setting. Visitors may enjoy panoramic views of the bay while eating typical Neapolitan delicacies like spaghetti alle vongole (clam pasta), fritto misto di mare (mixed seafood fry), and insalata di mare (seafood salad).

Posillipo's combination of natural beauty, historical charm, and private atmosphere makes it an ideal destination for travelers seeking a sumptuous vacation in Napoli. Whether you're enjoying the panoramic views from Parco Virgiliano, experiencing the underwater marvels of Gaiola Underwater Park, or indulging in gourmet seafood cuisine by the sea, Posillipo provides a genuinely memorable experience that encapsulates Napoli's coastal attraction.

The Spanish Quarter

The Spanish Quarter, also known as Quartieri Spagnoli in Italian, is one of Naples' most famous and energetic neighborhoods, distinguished by its tiny alleys, colorful buildings, and bustling atmosphere. The Spanish Quarter, steeped in history and culture, is a melting pot of customs, flavors, and experiences reflecting Napoli's rich and varied background. Here's a deeper look at what you can anticipate when you visit the Spanish Quarter.

Historical Background:
The Spanish Quarter was established in the 16th century to house Spanish troops stationed in Naples under the Spanish Vicerealm. Over the ages, the neighborhood has grown into a vibrant community noted for its close-knit social fabric and strong sense of identity.

Narrow Streets and Alleys:
The Spanish Quarter is known for its convoluted network of small streets, lanes, and stairs that meander through the neighborhood's closely packed buildings. Visitors may walk through these delightful alleys, enjoying the colorful facades, laundry hanging to dry, and vibrant street life.

Local Markets and Shops:
The Spanish Quarter is home to a variety of local markets, stores, and street vendors that offer anything from fresh vegetables and seafood to apparel, household items, and souvenirs. Visitors may immerse themselves in the vivid hustle and bustle of everyday life, bartering with merchants and enjoying local cuisine.

Street Art and Murals:
The Spanish Quarter is well-known for its thriving street art culture, which includes colorful murals on many of its walls and buildings. These creative expressions vary from political declarations and social criticism to abstract designs and amusing pictures, all contributing to the neighborhood's lively and unique atmosphere.

Cultural Diversity:
The Spanish Quarter is home to a varied group of inhabitants, including immigrants from all over Italy and beyond. This ethnic mix is mirrored in the neighborhood's culinary scene, which includes a variety of restaurants, trattorias, and pizzerias providing both traditional Neapolitan food and cosmopolitan flavors.

Local Cuisine and Dining:
The Spanish Quarter is a foodie's dream, with several restaurants, cafés, and street food booths serving traditional Neapolitan cuisine at reasonable costs. Visitors may enjoy typical dishes like pizza fritta (fried pizza), pasta al ragù, and sfogliatelle (Italian pastries) while taking in the bustling ambiance of the neighborhood.

Historical Landmarks:
 Visitors visiting the Spanish Quarter may see various ancient sites, including the Church of Sant'Anna di Palazzo, the Basilica of Santa Maria della Neve, and the Piazza del Mercato. These architectural marvels provide views into the neighborhood's rich history and religious traditions.

The Spanish Quarter in Napoli is a lively and energetic neighborhood that provides a really authentic Napoli experience. Whether you're exploring its small alleyways, experiencing its gastronomic pleasures, or admiring its colorful street art, the Spanish Quarter encourages you to immerse yourself in the cultural tapestry of Naples' busy center.

SANITA

Sanità, located northeast of Napoli's city center, is an area rich in history, culture, and a lively local community. Here's a thorough look at what makes Sanità a unique and fascinating part of Napoli:

Historical Significance:
Sanità boasts a rich past going back centuries. Once outside the city walls, it was a country area known for its lush grass and clean air, drawing royalty and lords who built great houses and castles here. Over time, Sanità became heavily settled, with the construction of apartment buildings to support the growing population. Today, relics of its noble past merge with the everyday life of its people.

Baroque building:
One of Sanità's main features is its beautiful Baroque building. The Basilica of Santa Maria della Sanità stands as a witness to this style, with its ornate entrance covered with detailed marble carvings and sculptures. Throughout the neighborhood, tourists can enjoy other Baroque churches, castles, and historic buildings, each adding to Sanità's architectural appeal.

Catacombs of San Gennaro:
The Catacombs of San Gennaro, a network of underground grave sites, are an important historical and religious place in Sanità. Dating back to the 2nd century AD, these tombs hold religious and historical importance, bringing tourists interested in exploring Napoli's early Christian past.

Local Markets and Shops:
Sanità is known for its busy street markets, giving a glimpse into daily life in Napoli. Visitors can explore stands offering fresh fruit, clothes, home goods, and local favorites, soaking themselves in the lively atmosphere of the neighborhood. These markets provide a chance to connect with locals, try traditional foods, and experience the original tastes of Napoli.

Botanical Garden of Naples:
The Botanical Garden of Naples, located on the edges of Sanità, offers a peaceful break from the busy city streets. Established in the 18th century, this botanical park is home to a diverse collection of plant species from around the world, providing a quiet oasis for tourists to explore.

Cultural Diversity and Community Spirit:
Sanità is a mixing pot of countries and practices, showing Napoli's rich history. Its tight-knit community is known for its kindness, resilience, and strong sense of identity. Throughout the year, Sanità hosts cultural events, holidays, and religious gatherings that bring residents together, creating a sense of unity and connection.

Local Cuisine and Dining:
Visitors to Sanità can indulge in real Neapolitan food at traditional trattorias, pizzerias, and cafes spread throughout the neighborhood. From wood-fired pizzas and pasta meals to seafood favorites and sweet treats, there's something to please every palate in Sanità.

Sanità captures the spirit of Napoli, with its rich history, artistic beauty, lively community, and culinary treats. Whether visiting its historic buildings, shopping at local markets, or simply soaking up the neighborhood's atmosphere, tourists are sure to be charmed by the beauty and character of Sanità.

CHAPTER 4: ICONIC LANDMARKS AND HIDDEN GEMS

Napoli, a city steeped in history and culture, is a treasure trove of iconic landmarks and hidden gems waiting to be discovered. From ancient ruins and grand palaces to charming neighborhoods and hidden oases, Napoli offers a captivating tapestry of experiences that captivate the imagination and stir the soul. Here's a comprehensive guide to some of the most notable landmarks and hidden gems in this vibrant Italian city:

Iconic Landmarks

Piazza del Plebiscito:

Piazza del Plebiscito is one of Naples' most recognisable and majestic squares, representing the city's rich history, cultural relevance, and architectural majesty. This enormous and beautiful square, located in the center of Naples, captivates tourists with its colossal structures, gorgeous façade, and dynamic atmosphere. Here's a closer look at Piazza del Plebiscito.

Historical Significance:
Piazza del Plebiscito is historically noteworthy since it has seen crucial occasions in Napoli's history. It was called after the referendum conducted in 1860, which resulted in the unification of Italy and the formation of the Kingdom of Italy. Over the years, the area has acted as a rallying place for political meetings, festivities, and cultural events. The area is surrounded by architectural marvels that merge neoclassical and Renaissance styles.

Royal Palace of Naples (Palazzo Reale):
The Palazzo Reale, with its towering façade and commanding presence, occupies one side of the Piazza. Originally a royal home, it currently contains museums and galleries that highlight Napoli's royal history and cultural legacy.

Basilica of San Francesco di Paola:
The Basilica of San Francesco di Paola, a beautiful neoclassical basilica inspired by Rome's Pantheon, overlooks the Palazzo Reale. Its towering colonnades and dome contribute to the grandeur of Piazza del Plebiscito, drawing tourists from all around.

Piazza del Plebiscito is a cultural center that hosts concerts, festivals, and public events year-round. From music concerts and art exhibits to political protests and religious processions, the area is alive with activity, attracting both residents and visitors.

The area provides panoramic views of Napoli's prominent sites, such as the Castel Nuovo, Bay of Napoli, and Mount Vesuvius. Visitors may enjoy these stunning views while wandering across the plaza or reclining on the spacious stairs.

Local Flavor:
The plaza is surrounded by cafés, restaurants, and stores, offering tourists a taste of Napoli's bustling street life. Piazza del Plebiscito, whether you're sipping a typical Neapolitan espresso or indulging in gelato, provides a flavor of Naples' gastronomic legacy.

Piazza del Plebiscito exemplifies Napoli's rich history, architectural splendor, and cultural life. Visitors are drawn by the grandeur of this historic plaza, whether they are admiring its colossal structures, soaking up its bustling atmosphere, or just enjoying the panoramic vistas.

Castel Nuovo

Castel Nuovo, also known as Maschio Angioino, is an outstanding medieval castle that stands majestically along the shoreline of Napoli, Italy. With its high towers, gorgeous façade, and rich history, Castel Nuovo is not only a reminder of Napoli's past but also a tribute to its ongoing cultural legacy. Here's a closer look at this historic landmark:

Historical Significance:
Castel Nuovo was established in the 13th century under the reign of Charles I of Anjou, thus its other name "Maschio Angioino," which means "Angevin Keep." It functioned as a royal home and a center of power for the Angevin dynasty, playing a crucial role in Napoli's political and social life for centuries.

Architectural Splendor:
The castle's architecture is a beautiful example of medieval military defenses blended with Renaissance elements. Its huge stone walls, fortified towers, and crenelated battlements represent the defensive capabilities of the age, while its exquisite courtyards, large halls, and intricate decorations exhibit the creative brilliance of Renaissance Italy.

Key Features:

Towers:
Castel Nuovo is recognisable by its four conspicuous towers, each with its own distinct character and function. The Torre di Mezzo (Middle Tower) and the Torre di Guardia (Watchtower) are among the most outstanding elements of the castle, affording panoramic views of Napoli and the surrounding region.

Triumphal Arch:
The majestic Arco di Trionfo (Triumphal Arch), embellished with sculptural reliefs and artistic elements, serves as the principal entrance to the castle. Built to

celebrate Alfonso I of Aragon's triumphant arrival into Napoli in 1443, the arch is a masterpiece of Renaissance workmanship and symbolism.

Courtyards and Halls:
Within the castle, tourists may explore a succession of courtyards, halls, and chambers that give insights into Napoli's history and culture. Highlights include the Sala dei Baroni (Barons' Hall), covered with murals representing episodes from the Angevin era, and the Cappella Palatina (Palatine Chapel), exhibiting outstanding medieval and Renaissance artworks.

Cultural Center:
Today, Castel Nuovo operates as a cultural center and museum, presenting exhibits, events, and performances that highlight Napoli's creative and historical history. Visitors may dig into the castle's rich history with guided tours, interactive exhibitions, and multimedia presentations that bring its fabled past to life.

Scenic Views:
One of the pleasures of visiting Castel Nuovo is the panoramic views it gives of the Bay of Napoli, the city skyline, and the spectacular Mount Vesuvius in the distance. From the castle's battlements and turrets, tourists may marvel at these stunning panoramas while immersing themselves in Napoli's timeless enchantment.

Castel Nuovo, with its towering presence and rich history, serves as a tribute to Napoli's continuing heritage and cultural relevance. Whether exploring its ancient halls, admiring its architectural beauty, or soaking in its panoramic vistas, tourists cannot help but be attracted by the ageless allure of this historic relic

The Palazzo Reale Di Capodimonte

The Palazzo Reale di Capodimonte, perched on a hill overlooking Napoli, Italy, is a beautiful royal palace that stands as a tribute to the city's rich history, artistic legacy, and cultural importance. Built in the 18th century as a royal home for the Bourbon monarchs of Naples, the palace offers grandeur, elegance, and architectural brilliance that continues to enchant tourists from across the globe. Here's a closer look at the Palazzo Reale di Capodimonte:

Historical Significance:
The Palazzo Reale di Capodimonte was commissioned by King Charles VII of Naples (later King Charles III of Spain) in the 1730s as a hunting lodge and summer palace for the Bourbon kings. Over the years, it blossomed into a prominent royal palace and cultural center, holding sumptuous banquets, receptions, and artistic gatherings that exhibited Napoli's lively cultural scene.

Architectural Grandeur:
Designed by the architect Giovanni Antonio Medrano, the Palazzo Reale di Capodimonte is a masterpiece of Neoclassical design. Its massive exterior, beautiful colonnades, and magnificent domes convey grandeur and refinement, reflecting the luxury and splendor of the Bourbon court.

Artistic Treasures:
The palace is known for its enormous collection of art and antiquities, which span centuries and represent a broad variety of styles and genres. The centerpiece of the collection is the Farnese Gallery, which comprises works by famous painters such as Titian, Raphael, Caravaggio, and El Greco. Additionally, the palace holds an astonishing assortment of sculptures, tapestries, furniture, and ornamental arts that provide insight into Napoli's rich cultural legacy.

National Museum of Capodimonte:
Today, the Palazzo Reale di Capodimonte functions as the National Museum of Capodimonte, home of one of Italy's most significant art collections. Visitors may tour the museum's enormous galleries and exhibition rooms, marveling at works of art from the Renaissance to the current day. Highlights include the classic Veiled Christ by Giuseppe Sanmartino, as well as works by renowned painters such as Botticelli, Michelangelo, and Caravaggio.

Scenic Surroundings:
Set between extensive parklands and lush gardens, the Palazzo Reale di Capodimonte provides spectacular views of Napoli and the surrounding countryside. Visitors may meander around the royal grounds, viewing groomed lawns, vivid flower beds, and quiet fountains while taking in the splendor of Napoli's natural surroundings.

Cultural Center:
In addition to its art collections, the Palazzo Reale di Capodimonte presents a range of cultural events, exhibits, and educational programs that reflect Napoli's creative tradition and cultural diversity. From temporary exhibits and lectures to music concerts and workshops, the palace serves as a lively center of cultural activity that improves the lives of tourists and locals alike.

The Palazzo Reale di Capodimonte serves as a tribute to Napoli's rich history, artistic tradition, and cultural vibrancy. Whether exploring its magnificent interiors, appreciating its world-class art collections, or just enjoying the picturesque surroundings, visitors can not help but be captured by the ageless charm of this stately royal castle.

The Catacombs of San Gennaro, located under the streets of Napoli, Italy, are a fascinating maze of subterranean burial places that provide an insight into the city's early Christian history and religious traditions. These catacombs, named for San Gennaro, Napoli's cherished patron saint, are a holy and spiritual pilgrimage site for believers, as well as an enticing destination for tourists looking to learn about the city's historic history. Here's an inside look at the Catacombs of San Gennaro:

Historical Significance:
The Catacombs of San Gennaro are one of Italy's oldest and largest catacomb complexes, dating back to the 2nd century AD. Originally utilized as burial grounds for early Christians, they became places of reverence and pilgrimage after the martyrdom of San Gennaro, who was buried here in the fifth century AD.

Architectural Features:
The catacombs are subterranean tunnels, chambers, and galleries cut from the soft volcanic rock under Napoli's streets. Visitors may navigate multiple levels of interconnecting corridors filled with antique murals, exquisite mosaics, and artistic motifs depicting biblical themes and Christian symbolism.

San Gennaro's Tomb:
At the heart of the catacombs is the tomb of San Gennaro, where the saint's relics are said to be deposited. Devotees and pilgrims throng to this hallowed spot to pay tribute to San Gennaro and seek his graces, particularly during religious festivals and feast days honoring the saint.

Christian Burials and Practices:
Early Christians believed in the resurrection of the corpse and used the Catacombs of San Gennaro for burial rather than cremation. The catacombs include hundreds of niches, known as loculi, where the dead were buried, frequently with burial inscriptions, symbols, and artifacts.

Religious Worship and Pilgrimage:
The Catacombs of San Gennaro have long been recognised as hallowed locations for prayer, devotion, and pilgrimage. Believers flock here to seek spiritual consolation, pray, and honor San Gennaro, who is said to protect Napoli and its people by his miraculous interventions.

The Catacombs of San Gennaro now provide guided tours for tourists to explore the subterranean pathways, learn about early Christian burial customs, and learn about the site's rich history and religious importance. Guided tours reveal the catacombs' archaeological value, artistic history, and cultural legacy, providing visitors with a one of a kind and immersive experience.

The Catacombs of San Gennaro are a tribute to Napoli's historic Christian past and spiritual devotion, encouraging tourists to plunge into the city's rich history and discover the hallowed depths under its streets. Whether seeking refuge in prayer, admiring ancient art, or just following in the footsteps of early Christians, a visit to the Catacombs of San Gennaro is a journey through time and religion that makes a lasting effect on all who enter.

Spaccanapoli

Spaccanapoli, literally "Naples splitter," is a historic roadway that slices across the heart of Napoli's old city, splitting it into two different halves. This busy avenue, also known as Via Benedetto Croce, is more than simply a street; it's a pulsating artery that pulsates with Napoli's rich history, cultural legacy, and daily life. Here's a closer look at Spaccanapoli:

Historical Significance:
Spaccanapoli has profound roots that extend back to ancient times when it was part of the Greek and Roman street system of Neapolis, the city's historical progenitor. Over the years, it grew into a busy commercial avenue and a focus of cultural and social activity, seeing the rise and fall of empires, the ebb and flow of commerce, and the rhythms of everyday life in Napoli.

Architectural Marvels:
Wandering throughout Spaccanapoli is like taking a voyage through Napoli's architectural past. The boulevard is surrounded by an eclectic collection of buildings, churches, and palaces that span many architectural styles, from medieval to baroque, neoclassical to Renaissance. Each building reveals a narrative of Napoli's history, with beautiful façade,

complex features, and secret courtyards waiting to be uncovered.

Religious Landmarks:
Spaccanapoli is home to various historic churches and religious landmarks that represent the city's rich spiritual traditions. The Church of Gesù Nuovo, with its characteristic front studded with diamond-shaped stones, and the Church of Santa Chiara, noted for its tranquil cloister and exquisite majolica-tiled seats, are just two examples of the architectural marvels that line the street.

Artisan Workshops and Boutiques:
One of the beauties of Spaccanapoli is its lively street life and busy business activities. Along the Boulevard, tourists will discover a multitude of artisan workshops, boutiques, and traditional stores offering anything from handcrafted crafts and artisanal items to local delicacies and souvenirs. It's the ideal spot to pick up a unique remembrance of your stay in Napoli.

Cultural Hub:
Spaccanapoli isn't simply a street; it's a cultural hub where Napoli's artistic and creative soul flourishes. Throughout the year, the street holds festivals, art exhibits, and cultural events that highlight the city's dynamic cultural environment and showcase the skills of local artists, musicians, and performers. From street art to live music, there's always something going along Spaccanapoli.

Local Flavor:

No vacation to Spaccanapoli would be complete without enjoying Napoli's gastronomic pleasures. The street is studded with classic trattorias, pizzerias, and cafés where tourists can enjoy real Neapolitan cuisine, from wood-fired pizzas and pasta meals to street food nibbles and sweet sweets. It's the best approach to immerse yourself in Napoli's gastronomic history. Spaccanapoli is more than simply a street; it's a living, breathing reflection of Napoli's rich history, cultural variety, and dynamic energy. Whether you're exploring its architectural wonders, shopping at its artisan stores, or relishing its gastronomic pleasures, Spaccanapoli welcomes you to experience the true spirit of Napoli in all its grandeur.

Via San Gregorio Armeno

Via San Gregorio Armeno, in the center of Napoli, Italy, is a short street known for its artisan workshops and stores that specialize in presepi, or nativities. Via San Gregorio Armeno, sometimes known as "Christmas Alley," is a lively road that comes alive with bustle, particularly during the holiday season. Take a closer look at this historic street.

Historical Significance:
Via San Gregorio Armeno has centuries of history. The street, named after the adjacent Church of San Gregorio Armeno, which was founded in the 10th century, has long been a hub for artisanal workmanship and religious devotion. It has become associated with the craft of presepi making throughout time, bringing people from all over the world.

Along Via San Gregorio Armeno, tourists may find several artisan studios and businesses specializing in presepi and related crafts. Skilled artists diligently manufacture complex figures, small structures, and elaborate dioramas portraying scenes from the Christmas story, as well as historical, cultural, and modern topics.

The history of building presepi, or nativity scenes, may be traced back to the 13th century in Italy. Naples, with its rich cultural past and strong religious traditions, has long been acclaimed for its intricate and realistic presepi. This practice is centered in Via San Gregorio Armeno, with artists carrying on the presepi making history handed down through centuries.

Year-Round Attraction:
While Via San Gregorio Armeno is best famed for its presepi workshops, it is also a vibrant attraction year round. Visitors may wander around the street's unusual mix of stores offering handcrafted products such as classic Neapolitan pottery, handmade souvenirs, and religious artifacts. It's ideal for finding one of a kind presents and mementos to remember your trip to Napoli.

Christmas Atmosphere:
During the holiday season, Via San Gregorio Armeno comes alive with festive decorations, dazzling lights, and the aroma of freshly baked pastries and mulled wine. The roadway transforms into a thriving outdoor market, with sellers selling Christmas decorations, ornaments, and other holiday themed merchandise. It's a lovely time to come and enjoy the pleasure and warmth of the season.

Cultural Experience:
Exploring Via San Gregorio Armeno is more than simply shopping; it's also a chance to learn about Napoli's artistic and religious traditions. Visitors may observe artists at work, learn about the history of presepi-making, and soak in the vivid ambiance of this one of a kind street.

Via San Gregorio Armeno is a must-see for anybody visiting Naples, providing a fascinating peek into the city's artistic and cultural past. A journey around Via San Gregorio Armeno is guaranteed to be a remarkable experience, whether you're shopping for souvenirs, appreciating the skill of local craftsmen, or just taking in the festive atmosphere.

The Galleria Umberto I

The Galleria Umberto I, located in the center of Naples, Italy, is an attractive and ancient retail arcade that emanates grandeur, elegance, and architectural splendor. Built in the late nineteenth century during the Belle Époque period, this spectacular glass-roofed gallery is a cultural monument and a symbol of Napoli's rich history, creative legacy, and international flair. Here's a closer look at Galleria Umberto I.

Historical Background:
Architect Emanuele Rocco conceived and built the Galleria Umberto I from 1887 to 1891. It was named in honor of Umberto I, the King of Italy at the time, and was designed to be a prominent shopping destination and social meeting place for Napoli's elite.

The Galleria Umberto I, a masterwork of architectural design, has a towering glass dome, sweeping ironwork, and luxurious interiors. Inspired by other famous European retail arcades, such as Milan's Galleria Vittorio Emanuele II, the gallery has a symmetrical arrangement with two major crossing halls packed with fine stores, cafés, and restaurants.

The Galleria Umberto I exudes grandeur and splendor, evoking a bygone period of wealth and elegance. The gallery's marble floors, elegant balconies, and detailed craftsmanship provide a luxurious setting for shopping, eating, and socializing, reflecting the grandeur and refinement of Belle Époque Napoli.

Cultural Hub:
Galleria Umberto I has long been a gathering spot for both residents and tourists. Since its founding, it has held a wide range of cultural events, exhibits, and performances, including art displays, fashion presentations, musical concerts, and theatrical productions. The gallery continues to draw artists, musicians, and performers who contribute to its thriving cultural landscape.

Shopping and Dining:
The Galleria Umberto I has a variety of stores, boutiques, and luxury brands, including haute couture apparel, designer accessories, gourmet delights, and specialized items. Visitors may go shopping, peruse the newest trends, or just observe the magnificent displays and window decorations that line the gallery's stores. In addition, the gallery has a variety of cafés, restaurants,

and pastry shops where tourists may sample wonderful Italian food and gastronomic pleasures.

Iconic Landmark:
The Galleria Umberto I is an architectural gem that showcases Napoli's rich history, cultural legacy, and cosmopolitan character. Whether admiring its towering dome, perusing its beautiful halls, or going shopping, a visit to the Galleria Umberto I provides a peek of Napoli's everlasting attractiveness during the Belle Époque period.

To summarize, the Galleria Umberto I is more than simply a retail mall; it is a cultural institution, a historical monument, and a representation of Napoli's continuing elegance and refinement. Visitors to this spectacular gallery are fascinated by its ageless beauty and grandeur, whether they are wandering through its luxurious interiors, savoring delicious food, or just soaking in the atmosphere.

HIDDEN GEMS

Fontenelle Cemetery

An intriguing burial site constructed into the tuff rock under Napoli's streets. Fontanelle Cemetery has hundreds of skeleton remains and acts as a unique tribute to the city's horrific heritage.

Villa Floridana

A tranquil park situated atop Vomero Hill, affording panoramic views of the city and harbor. Villa Floridiana is a secret oasis where tourists may escape from the rush and bustle of Napoli's streets and enjoy a leisurely walk among lush flora.

Napoli Sotterranea (Underground)

A network of tunnels, vaults, and chambers buried under Napoli's streets, providing a fascinating look into the city's historic history. Guided tours in Napoli Sotterranea give information about the city's history, architecture, and culture.

The Santa Chiara Cloister

A tranquil haven nestled in the middle of Napoli's old town, with a verdant garden, amazing ceramic tilework, and a pleasant attitude. Santa Chiara Cloister is a hidden gem where visitors may escape the city's bustle and immerse themselves in beauty and serenity.

Villa Doria D'Angri

A lovely medieval palace surrounded by lush gardens and stunning views, delivering a tranquil respite from Napoli's metropolitan bustle. Villa Doria d'Angri is a hidden treasure where guests may relax in the peace of nature while taking panoramic views of the city and harbor.

Sansevero Chapel (Calle Sansevero)

A magnificent baroque church famous for its outstanding marble statues, notably Giuseppe Sanmartino's Veiled Christ. Sansevero Chapel is a hidden treasure of art and architecture, presenting tourists with insight into Napoli's creative heritage and spiritual dedication.

Napoli's major sites and hidden secrets enable tourists to discover its rich history, lively culture, and timeless beauty. Whether meandering through medieval streets, marveling at Baroque masterpieces, or exploring a secret oasis of solitude, Napoli delivers a fully immersive and exciting experience for all travelers.

CHAPTER 5: MOUTHWATERING CUISINE AND DINING EXPERIENCES

Napoli, known for its rich culinary legacy and delicious cuisine, offers a diverse range of dining experiences that will delight even the most discerning palate. From traditional Neapolitan dinners full of flavor to modern inventions that push the boundaries of gastronomy, Napoli's culinary scene is a feast for the senses. Nepal's cuisine is unique, emphasizing fresh ingredients, powerful flavors, and balanced nutrition.

In this chapter, I'll take you on a tour of Napoli's eating scene, looking at the city's most famous dishes as well as hidden culinary gems. We will delve into the history of Nepalese cuisine and the cultural significance of its dishes. For visitors looking for a more upscale dining experience, Napoli has numerous top-tier restaurants, several of which have Michelin stars.

So prepare to go on a gastronomic journey across Napoli's bustling culinary scene. Whether you are a gourmet or just want to learn about the local culture via its food, Napoli offers something for everyone.

Neapolitan Pizza

Neapolitan pizza has a particular place in the hearts and stomachs of food enthusiasts all around the globe, and for good reason. This classic dish, which originated in Naples, represents the city's rich culinary legacy and customs. Here's a deeper look at what makes Neapolitan pizza so special.

Authentic Ingredients:
Neapolitan pizza is made with a few basic yet high-quality ingredients that embody the idea of Italian cuisine. The dough is composed of wheat flour, water, salt, and yeast, resulting in a soft and chewy crust with a slightly burnt outside. San Marzano tomatoes cultivated in the volcanic soil of Campania are used to make the colorful tomato sauce, and fresh buffalo mozzarella cheese gives a creamy texture and rich taste.

Wood-Fired Oven:
The traditional wood-fired oven, also known as a "forno a legna," is a vital component of Neapolitan pizza. These ovens can achieve very high temperatures, usually over 800°F (430°C), enabling

the pizza to cook rapidly and uniformly. The extreme heat produces the distinctive leopard-spotted char on the crust while also giving a smoky taste to the toppings.

Severe Requirements:
To be called genuine Neapolitan pizza, the pizza must follow the severe requirements established by the Associazione Verace Pizza Napoletana. These criteria encompass everything from the pizza's size and form to the ingredients and technique of cooking. For example, Neapolitan pizza must have a circumference of no more than 35 centimeters and a crust no thicker than 1-2 cm.

Cultural Heritage:
Neapolitan pizza is a cultural heritage recognized by UNESCO. In 2017, UNESCO added the "Art of Neapolitan 'Pizzaiuoli'" to its list of Intangible Cultural Heritage, recognizing the centuries-old history and artistry behind this famous culinary dish.

Served with Tradition:
In Naples, eating pizza is more than simply a culinary experience; it is also a social and cultural one. Pizzerias are vibrant meeting places where friends and family may enjoy a meal and celebrate

life. In Naples, the ritual of eating pizza frequently includes pulling off pieces by hand, savoring each mouthful, and washing it down with a drink of local wine or beer.

Neapolitan pizza is more than a meal; it represents Napoli's enthusiasm, passion, and dedication to preserve its culinary history for future generations. So, the next time you visit Naples, make sure to have a piece of true Neapolitan pizza and feel the enchantment for yourself.

Seafood specialist

Napoli's coastal location gives it an excess of fresh fish, which plays a key role in the city's culinary scene. Here's a mouthwatering look at some of the seafood treats you can savor in Napoli:

Spaghetti alle Vongole (Spaghetti with Clams): This famous Neapolitan dish features soft clams sautéed with garlic, olive oil, white wine, and chili flakes, then tossed with al dente spaghetti. It's a simple yet tasty pasta dish that perfectly shows the freshness of the fish.

Frittura di Pesce (Mixed Fried Seafood): Napoli's frittura di pesce is a mouthwatering mix of fried seafood, including shrimp, calamari, small fish, and sometimes even octopus or shellfish. The seafood is covered in a light batter and fried to golden perfection, resulting in a crispy and delicious treat.

Baccalà (Salted Cod):
While not exclusive to Napoli, baccalà holds a special place in Neapolitan food. The salted cod is rehydrated, then usually cooked in a variety of ways, such as stewed with tomatoes, olives, and capers, or fried and served with a squeeze of lemon. It's a filling and rich dish that goes nicely with warm bread.

Scialatielli ai Frutti di Mare (Fresh Pasta with Mixed Seafood): Scialatielli is a type of fresh pasta similar to fettuccine, often made with flour, water, and sometimes eggs. In this dish, scialatielli is tossed with a rich seafood sauce made from a variety of fresh shellfish, such as mussels, clams, shrimp, and squid, cooked in a tomato-based sauce flavored with garlic, white wine, and fresh herbs.

Insalata di Mare (Seafood Salad):
Insalata di mare is a delicious and lively seafood salad featuring a mix of cooked and preserved seafood, such as shrimp, squid, octopus, mussels,

and scallops, tossed with lemon juice, olive oil, garlic, parsley, and sometimes capers or olives. It's a light and delicious starter or antipasto that's great for a hot summer day.

Grilled Fish:
Napoli's coastal setting means that fresh fish is numerous and often grilled to perfection. Whether it's whole fish like branzino (sea bass) or pesce spada (swordfish), or pieces of bream, mullet, or sole, grilled fish is a simple yet delicious way to enjoy the natural tastes of the sea.

From pasta meals filled with seafood to simple grilled fish, Napoli's seafood specialties showcase the region's culinary skill and the bounty of the Mediterranean Sea. Buon appetito!

Street food Delights

Napoli's lively street food scene is a gastronomic experience waiting to be discovered. Here are some appealing street cuisine pleasures to sample when visiting the city:

Pizza Fritta (fried pizza):
Pizza fritta is a popular Neapolitan street snack made with deep-fried dough that is then packed with a variety of savory contents such as tomato

sauce, mozzarella cheese, ricotta, salami, and vegetables. It's a delicious and rich treat ideal for on-the-go nibbling.

Arancini:
Golden, deep-fried rice balls are a popular street food snack in Naples. Arancini, filled with a savory blend of rice, ragù (meat sauce), peas, and mozzarella cheese, are flavorful and make for a wonderful and portable lunch or snack.

Cuoppo di Mare (Fried Seafood Cone):
A cone-shaped container packed with a variety of fried seafood, including shrimp, calamari, tiny fish, and sometimes vegetables like zucchini or eggplant. Cuoppo di mare, the ultimate street food treat for seafood lovers, is crispy, delicious, and very gratifying.

Sfogliatella:
Sfogliatella, Napoli's signature pastry, is a must-try street food delicacy. This flaky, shell-shaped pastry has a sweet and creamy ricotta filling scented with citrus zest, candied fruit, or cinnamon. Sfogliatella may be served warm or at room temperature, making it an ideal sweet treat to savor while visiting the city.

Panini con la Porchetta (Porchetta Sandwich): The panino con la porchetta is a simple but tasty street food classic in Naples, made with slices of delicate, roasted porchetta (pork belly) wrapped within a crusty bun and commonly served with a drizzle of olive oil and a sprinkling of salt. Crispy, aromatic pork and soft, chewy bread make for the ideal comfort meal.

Crocchè di Patate (Potato Croquettes): Crocchè di patate are crispy, golden-brown potato croquettes stuffed with creamy mashed potatoes, cheese, and sometimes ham or parsley. These delicious small pieces are the ideal street food snack to eat while roaming around the streets of Naples.

From savory fried snacks to sweet pastries, Napoli's street food offerings provide a fascinating sample of the city's culinary history and will leave you wanting more. Good appetite!

Dinner with a View

Dining with a view in Napoli is a really spectacular experience, combining delectable food with breathtaking views of the metropolis or the sparkling waters of the Bay of Naples. Here are some excellent alternatives for dining with a view in Naples:

Ristorante Caruso:
Perched atop Vomero Hill, Ristorante Caruso provides panoramic views of Napoli's ancient downtown and the spectacular Mount Vesuvius. Dine on classic Neapolitan food while admiring the stunning surroundings from the restaurant's patio, which makes an ideal setting for a romantic evening or special occasion.

La Terrazza dei Barbanti:
Located in Napoli's historic center, La Terrazza dei Barbanti provides panoramic views of Piazza del Gesù Nuovo and the renowned Spire of the Immaculate Virgin. Enjoy superb Mediterranean cuisine prepared with locally sourced ingredients while taking in the atmosphere of this ancient area.

Ristorante Marechiaro:
Located along the gorgeous Posillipo coastline, Ristorante Marechiaro offers breathtaking views of the Bay of Naples, Capri, and Ischia. Enjoy delicious seafood delights while watching the sun set over the Mediterranean Sea from the restaurant's patio, resulting in an amazing dining experience.

Terrazza Calabritto:
Situated in the vibrant Chiaia area, Terrazza Calabritto provides panoramic views of the Bay of Naples and the picturesque coastal promenade. Enjoy inventive Mediterranean food with a contemporary touch, complimented by a wonderful range of wines, while admiring the splendor of Napoli's coastline and skyline.

Ristorante palace Petrucci:
Set in a historic palace in the center of Napoli's old town, Ristorante Palazzo Petrucci provides a classy dining experience with views of Piazza San Domenico Maggiore and the Church of San Domenico. Enjoy new meals inspired by traditional Neapolitan cuisine while enjoying the architectural splendor of this ancient plaza.

Borgo Sant'Antonio Abate:
For a more relaxed eating experience with a view, visit Borgo Sant'Antonio Abate, a beautiful district in Naples' old center. Discover small trattorias and osterias situated among narrow alleyways and busy piazzas, where you can savor real Neapolitan food while immersing yourself in local culture and ambience.

Whether you're looking for a romantic supper for two or a memorable meal with friends and family, Napoli has a range of dining options with stunning views that will make an impact.

Traditional Trattorias

Traditional trattorias in Naples are legendary restaurants that provide traditional Neapolitan food in a pleasant and inviting setting. These restaurants are known for focusing on fresh, locally produced foods and time-honored traditions handed down through generations. When you visit a trattoria in Naples, you can expect to eat traditional meals like pasta e fagioli (pasta with beans), spaghetti alle vongole (spaghetti with clams), eggplant parmigiana, and, of course, the world-famous Neapolitan pizza. The atmosphere is frequently vibrant, with friendly service and rustic décor adding to the appeal. Whether you're a native or a guest, eating at a classic trattoria in Napoli is a unique experience that showcases the city's rich culinary legacy.

CHAPTER 6: ENGAGING CULTURAL EXPERIENCES

As I walked through the busy streets of Napoli, I couldn't help but wonder at the city's rich cultural history. Welcome to Napoli, a city where the sounds of ancient civilizations resonate through its cobblestone streets, where the aroma of freshly baked pizza fills the air, and where every corner holds a story waiting to be found. Nestled in the picturesque region of Campania in southern Italy, Napoli is a cultural gem that beckons visitors to engage themselves in its rich mix of history, art, food, and lively street life.

Engaging with the cultural events of Napoli is not merely a visit but a trip through time, giving a look into the city's famous past and lively present. From discovering historic sites that bear witness to millennia of civilization to enjoying the culinary delights that have charmed palates for centuries, Napoli promises an educational and memorable experience for every guest.

In this introduction, we will dive into the fascinating cultural landscape of Napoli, stressing its famous sites, artistic gems, culinary customs, and lively street scenes. Whether you are a history fan, an art aficionado, a food expert, or simply a curious tourist wanting to immerse yourself in the spirit of Napoli, this guide will serve as your partner in unlocking the city's vast cultural wealth. So, let us start on a trip of finding and adventure as we uncover the fascinating cultural experiences awaiting us in Napoli.

Exploring Historical Sites:
Exploring Napoli's ancient sites is like embarking on a captivating journey through time, with each cobblestone street and old building telling a story from decades ago. This lively city, nestled in the turquoise waters of the Bay of Naples, has a millennia-long history, leaving behind architectural marvels, archaeological wonders, and cultural riches.

Napoli's historic town is a UNESCO World Heritage Site, known for its winding streets, Baroque churches, and centuries-old palazzi. Visitors may stroll through the vibrant Spaccanapoli, a little street that runs through the ancient city like a spine, revealing a treasure trove of architectural beauties at each turn. Admire the splendor of the Duomo di Napoli, the city's greatest cathedral, with its stunning facade adorned with intricate reliefs and sculptures.

No tour of Napoli's old sights would be complete without a stop at the Castel Nuovo, or New Castle, a medieval castle that has guarded the city for over seven centuries. The Angevin dynasty built this magnificent fortress in the 13th century, and it has towering towers, elegant rooms, and a majestic triumphal arch, symbolizing Napoli's perseverance and grandeur. Travelers may get a glimpse of ancient Roman life by visiting Napoli's underground catacombs. The Catacombs of San Gennaro, named after the city's patron saint, provide a unique glimpse into early Christian burial rituals, with intricate passageways adorned with frescoes, sculptures, and ancient inscriptions. Of course, no trip to Naples is complete without seeing the nearby ancient sites of Pompeii and Herculaneum. These historic communities, frozen in time by Mount Vesuvius' cataclysmic eruption in 79 AD, offer a unique look into everyday Roman life, with well-preserved streets, dwellings, and public buildings that provide a vivid image of ancient civilization.

Artistic Treasures

Napoli, with its rich cultural legacy and illustrious past, is a treasure trove of artistic wonders that entice visitors from all over the globe. From

Renaissance masterpieces to modern works, the city's museums, galleries, and cathedrals showcase an extraordinary collection of cultural treasures that reflect Napoli's immense impact on the world of art. The Museo di Capodimonte, a magnificent Bourbon palace-turned-museum built on a hill overlooking the city, is one of Napoli's most important cultural assets. Visitors may see an extraordinary collection of paintings, sculptures, and decorative arts from the 13th to 18th centuries. Highlights include works by well-known painters such as Caravaggio, Titian, Raphael, and Masaccio, as well as a stunning collection of Neapolitan Baroque art by Luca Giordano and Francesco Solimena.

For individuals who like ancient art, the Museo Archeologico Nazionale is a must-see. This world-class museum, housed in a beautiful Bourbon castle in the heart of Napoli, has one of the world's most extensive collections of Roman artifacts, including stunning mosaics, sculptures, and paintings discovered at nearby archaeological sites such as Pompeii, Herculaneum, and Paestum. The Farnese Bull sculpture, Toro Farnese, and the beautiful Alexander Mosaic are among the museum's most notable artifacts.

In addition to its well-known museums, Napoli boasts a strong contemporary art scene, with galleries and cultural organizations presenting the work of young and recognised artists from Italy and beyond. The Museo d'Arte Contemporanea Donnaregina (MADRE) is a notable representative of contemporary art in Naples, housing a broad collection of painting, sculpture, photography, video, and installation art. The museum, built in a former 19th-century castle in the historic town, has rotating exhibits on subjects ranging from social and political issues to experimental forms of creative expression.

Beyond museums and galleries, Napoli's streets and piazzas serve as outdoor galleries, with bright murals, street art, and sculptures gracing public areas across the city. From the bright paintings of the Quartieri Spagnoli to the bizarre sculptures of the Lungomare Caracciolo, Napoli's urban environment is alive with imagination and inventiveness.

Sophisticated Treats

Nestled in the southern region of Italy, Napoli has a gastronomy scene as vibrant and rich as its historical legacy. Napoli is known for being the birthplace of pizza, but the city offers visitors much more than just this one dish. Its abundant vegetables, fresh seafood, and rich culinary history are highlighted, offering visitors an intriguing range of flavors, aromas, and culinary experiences.

Napoli is known for its pizza, which is the centerpiece of the city's culinary scene. It is made with simple but excellent ingredients that come together to produce a harmonious blend of flavors. The classic Neapolitan pizza, called pizza margherita, is made with a thin, chewy dough that is baked to perfection in a wood-fired oven and topped with buffalo mozzarella, fresh basil, San Marzano tomatoes, and extra-virgin olive oil. Tasted at a traditional pizzeria such as Da Michele or Sorbillo, or enjoyed on the go from a street vendor, Napoli's pizza is a culinary adventure not to be missed.

Napoli has plenty to offer in terms of culinary delights that showcase the region's skill and dedication to high-quality ingredients, in addition to pizza. A large portion of Neapolitan cuisine features seafood, with dishes like spaghetti alle vongole (spaghetti with clams), frittura di paranza (mixed fried seafood), and insalata di mare (seafood salad) highlighting the day's freshest catch. Pasta recipes like paccheri alla Genovese, or pasta with a thick meat and onion sauce, and spaghetti alla puttanesca, or spaghetti with tomatoes, olives, capers, and anchovies, on the other hand, highlight Napoli's rich culinary heritage and the influence of other cultural traditions.

Sfogliatelle, flaky pastries filled with ricotta cheese and candied fruit, panzerotti, or deep-fried rice balls, are just a few of the mouth watering street food options available in Napoli. Babà al rum, on the other hand, are rum-soaked sponge cakes. No trip to Napoli would be complete without sampling these delectable treats. Napoli's street food offerings are sure to tantalize the senses and provide a memorable experience, whether they are enjoyed in a traditional trattoria or while on-the-go from a neighborhood bakery.

One must visit Napoli's bustling markets in order to fully immerse oneself in the city's culinary culture. Residents congregate at the bustling Mercato di Porta Nolana and Mercato di Pignasecca to buy fresh fruit, cured meats, handmade cheeses, and other culinary delights. Here, visitors may sample local specialties, interact with vendors, and gain understanding of the many cooking customs that have shaped Napoli's culinary identity.

Bright Street Life

Nothing shows how intensely Napoli pulses more than its vibrant street life, which is really unique to the city. Napoli's streets are a visual feast of sights, sounds, and tastes that capture the essence of this dynamic city, from the bustling marketplaces and colorful piazzas to the colorful neighborhoods and busy thoroughfares. The vibrant markets that are the center of Napoli's street life are where locals and visitors alike go to make purchases, strike up conversations, and indulge in the cuisine of the city. Two of the city's most well-known markets, Mercato di Porta Nolana and Mercato di Pignasecca, provide an uncommon assortment of fresh fruit, seafood, meats, cheeses, and handcrafted goods. Visitors may peruse the bustling booths, sample local specialties, and get fully engrossed in the vibrant sights, sounds, and aromas of Napoli's culinary scene here.

The streets of Napoli are also home to a wide range of entertainers, artisans, and street performers that contribute to the vibrant ambiance of the city. Napoli's streets are a vibrant canvas where creativity abounds, from street artists creating stunning murals and colorful works of art to musicians serenading passersby with traditional Neapolitan sounds. Explore the winding alleyways of the Quartieri Spagnoli, where vibrant street art and bustling street markets create a dynamic atmosphere, or stroll down the popular promenades of Via Toledo and Via Chiaia, where shops, cafés and boutiques line the sidewalks.

To see Napoli's famous passeggiata, or twilight promenade, would be to miss the highlight of any visit to the city's street life. People travel to the streets to see and be seen as the sun sets and the city comes alive with bright lights and lively bustle. They engage in lively conversations, people-watch, and take in the vibrant ambiance of Napoli's streets. The passeggiata is a well-known Napoli custom that gives visitors a glimpse into the vibrant street life and rich cultural past of the city, whether they are strolling along the seaside promenade of Lungomare Caracciolo or exploring the historic passageways of the Centro Storico.

Cultural Festivals and Events

Napoli is not only a city with a rich history, captivating art, and delicious cuisine, but it is also a cultural hotspot, with a profusion of festivals and events celebrating its vibrant traditions and distinct heritage. Throughout the year, Napoli hosts a wide range of cultural festivities that allow visitors to immerse themselves in the city's dynamic cultural scene and experience its unique charm firsthand. The Feast of San Gennaro, which is held in September to honor the city's patron saint, is one of Napoli's most well-known cultural events. This religious holiday is distinguished by colorful processions, intricate ceremonies, and vivid street festivals that fill the city with music, dancing, and joy. Visitors may see the devotion to the saint's relics at the Duomo di Napoli, join in religious processions through the ancient neighborhoods, and taste traditional Neapolitan foods such as zeppole and sfogliatelle, which are enjoyed during the festivities.

In addition to religious celebrations, Napoli is known for its vibrant arts and entertainment scene, which includes a wide range of cultural festivals and events held throughout the year. The Napoli Teatro Festival, for example, showcases cutting-edge theater works from Italy and throughout the world, giving visitors the opportunity to see the best of contemporary theater in a variety of places around the city. Similarly, the Napoli Film Festival celebrates cinema by playing independent films, documentaries, and international films that represent Napoli's cultural diversity and artistic innovation.

Music also takes center stage in Napoli's cultural calendar, with a number of music festivals and concerts held throughout the year to showcase the city's rich musical legacy and thriving music scene. The Napoli Pizza Village, for example, combines music, food, and entertainment in a week-long celebration of Napoli's most famous culinary export, while the Napoli Pizza Jazz Festival offers a unique fusion of jazz music and Neapolitan cuisine in a series of concerts and performances at iconic venues throughout the city.

Finally, engaging with Napoli's cultural experiences is a journey of discovery and immersion in a city brimming with history, art, and culinary delights. Whether exploring its historic sites, indulging in its gastronomic richness, or just taking in the vibrant street life, Napoli provides travelers with an unforgettable experience.

CHAPTER 7: 7-DAY ITINERARY IN NAPOLI

A 7-Day Itinerary in Naples

Planning a 7-day itinerary in Napoli allows you to fully immerse yourself in the city's rich history, vibrant culture, delicious cuisine, and magnificent scenery. Here's a suggested itinerary to help you make the most of your visit in this fascinating city.

Day 1: Arrival and Historic Centre Exploration

Morning: Arrive in Napoli and check into your accommodation. Begin your adventure around the city by strolling through the historic center, a UNESCO World Heritage Site. Visit the Duomo di Napoli, San Gregorio Armeno (known for its nativity scene artisans), and the Spaccanapoli Boulevard.

Afternoon: Have a leisurely lunch at a typical trattoria, where you may savor local favorites like pizza margherita or pasta alla Genovese. After lunch, go deeper into Napoli's history by visiting the Napoli Underground Archaeological Museum or the Naples National Archaeological Museum.

Evening: Take a stroll along the Lungomare Caracciolo promenade to soak in the vibrant atmosphere of Napoli's street life, followed by dinner at a waterfront restaurant with spectacular views of the bay.

Day 2: Artistic treasures and Castel dell'Ovo

Morning: Start your day with a visit to the Museo di Capodimonte, which has an incredible collection of Renaissance and Baroque art. Marvel at Caravaggio, Titian, and Raphael's masterpieces.

After lunch, take a leisurely stroll around the Villa Comunale garden before seeing Castel dell'Ovo, a medieval castle constructed on a seaside promontory. Explore the castle grounds and take in the stunning views of the port and Mount Vesuvius.

Evening: Dine at a traditional seafood restaurant in the Chiaia district before taking a leisurely evening stroll along the lovely Via Chiaia, which is lined with boutiques, cafés, and gelaterias.

Day 3: Pompeii and Herculaneum excursion

Full Day:
Take a day journey to the ancient cities of Pompeii and Herculaneum, which were buried by Mount Vesuvius' explosion in 79 AD. Explore Pompeii's well-preserved ruins, which include a forum, amphitheater, and homes with frescoed walls. Then, visit Herculaneum's modest but equally impressive ruins, which include well preserved mosaics and murals.

Evening:
Return to Naples and unwind with dinner at a charming trattoria in the ancient town.

Day 4: Food Tour and Quartieri Spagnoli.

Morning:
Begin your day with a guided gourmet tour of Naples, where you'll sample local delights at markets, bakeries, and street food stalls. Discover the city's culinary delights by sampling fresh seafood, artisan cheeses, and classic pastries.

Afternoon:
Explore the stunning Quartieri Spagnoli neighborhood, known for its narrow streets, vibrant street art, and lively ambiance. Visit the Church of Santa Maria delle Grazie and meander along Via Toledo, one of the city's main thoroughfares.

Evening:
Have dinner at a traditional pizza restaurant in the Quartieri Spagnoli, followed by drinks at a bustling bar where you can engage with locals and soak up the neighborhood's vibrant atmosphere.

Day 5: Capri Island Tour

Full Day:
Take a boat from Napoli to the beautiful island of Capri, which is known for its magnificent coastline, crystal-clear waters, and opulent environment. Spend the day exploring the island's attractions, which include the Blue Grotto, Villa San Michele, and Augustus Gardens. Relax on one of Capri's stunning beaches and have a leisurely lunch at a seaside café.

Evening:
Return to Napoli and dine at a beautiful trattoria in the old center, with typical Neapolitan dishes such as eggplant parmigiana and pasta alle vongole.

Day 6: Vesuvius and Wine Tasting

Morning:
Take a guided tour of Mount Vesuvius, the famous volcano that towers above Naples. Hike to the crater rim for breathtaking views of the sea and the surrounding landscape.

After descending from Vesuvius, stop at a tiny vineyard in the adjacent region of Campania for a guided wine tasting. Pair regional wines such as Lacryma Christi and Aglianico with local cheeses, cured meats, and olive oil.

Evening:
Return to Napoli and have a last lunch at a famous trattoria, savoring the flavors of Campania once more.

Day 7: Departure

Morning:
Depending on your departure time, spend your last morning in Napoli relaxing in an old-town café, sipping espresso and eating pastries.

Afternoon:
Check out of your accommodation and transfer to the airport or train station for your next

destination, saying goodbye to Napoli with fond recollections of a magnificent week filled with history, art, food, and cultural contacts.

This itinerary offers a good balance of cultural exploration, culinary delights, and natural beauty, allowing you to explore the best of Napoli in only seven days. Adjustments may be made based on specific preferences and interests, ensuring a customized and unique experience in this busy metropolis.

CHAPTER 8: Practical Information and Tips About Napoli

Etiquette and Customs

Napoli's etiquette and customs are heavily influenced by tradition, reflecting the city's rich history, strong sense of community, and passionate spirit. Understanding and honoring local customs will help you enjoy your vacation and navigate Napoli's complicated cultural milieu with ease. Here are some important etiquette and norms to keep in mind while visiting Napoli:

Greetings and Politeness:
Neapolitans value civility and decency in social situations. When meeting someone for the first time or entering a business or restaurant, it is customary to greet them with a pleasant "buongiorno" (good morning) or "buonasera" (good evening), followed by a handshake or nod of the head. Saying "per favore" (please) and "grazie"

(thank you) are both meaningful expressions of respect and appreciation.

Personal Space and Gestures:
Neapolitans are known for their warm and expressive gestures, which are an essential part of communication. While speaking, you may see hand gestures such as waving, pointing, and gesturing with the fingers. However, it's critical to respect personal space and avoid invading someone's personal bubble, especially with new gestures.

Dress Code:
Napoli has a liberal dress code, however it is essential to dress appropriately for different occasions. When visiting churches or religious sites, both men and women should dress modestly, with shoulders and knees covered. Smart-casual attire is appropriate in more formal settings, such as luxury restaurants or cultural activities.

Mealtime Customs:
Food is an important part of Neapolitan culture, and meals are usually eaten as social gatherings with family and friends. When dining out, it is customary to wait for everyone to be served before starting to eat, and to keep your hands visible on the table while eating. When dining at someone's

home, it is customary to provide a little gift for the host, such as a bottle of wine or a dessert.

Respect for Seniors:
Respect for the elderly is deeply embedded in Neapolitan culture. Seniors are usually addressed with titles such as "signora" (Mrs.) or "signore" (Mr.), followed by their last name. When interacting with elders or persons in positions of authority, it is essential to show consideration and respect.

Socialise and Community:
Neapolitans are known for their sense of community and friendliness. It is normal to strike up conversations with strangers, especially in public places like cafés and piazzas. Throughout your time in Napoli, interact with others, seek advice, and be willing to form new connections.

Street Etiquette:
When walking through Napoli's congested streets, it's important to keep aware of your surroundings and follow common-sense safety practices. When crossing the street, be aware of vehicles, use pedestrian crossings, and avoid jaywalking. Keep valuables safe and use caution in crowded areas, especially tourist destinations.

By following these manners and customs in Naples, you may demonstrate respect for the city's culture and traditions while enjoying a memorable and enjoyable experience. Accept the warmth and generosity of the Neapolitans, immerse yourself in the native way of life, and discover the unique appeal of this bustling city.

Simple Language Phrases to know in Napoli

When visiting Napoli, despite English being frequently spoken and understood, learning some basic Italian words will considerably improve your experience and help you explore the city with ease. Here are some easy language phrases to know:

Greetings:
Buongiorno (BWON-jor-no) - Good morning
Buonasera (BWOH-nah-seh-rah) - Good evening
Ciao (CHOW) - Hello/Hi/Goodbye (informal)

Politeness:
Per favore (pair FAH-vor-reh) - Please
Grazie (GRAH-tsyeh) - Thank you
Prego (PREH-goh) - You're welcome

Basic Communication:
Sì (SEE) - Yes
No (NOH) - No
Scusa (SKOO-zah) - Excuse me/Sorry (informal)
Mi dispiace (mee dee-SPYAH-cheh) - I'm sorry

Asking for Help:
Dove? (DOH-veh) - Where?
Posso aiutarti? (POH-ssoh ah-YOO-tar-tee) - Can I assist you?
Parli inglese? (PAR-lee een-GLEH-zeh) - Do you speak English?

Directions:
Destra (DEHS-trah) - Right
Sinistra (seen-EES-trah) - Left
Dritto (DREE-toh) - Straight ahead
Vicino (vee-CHEE-noh) - Near
Lontano (lon-TAH-noh) - Far

Ordering Food and Drinks:
Vorrei... (vohr-RAY) - I would want...
Un caffè, per favore (oon kah-FEH, pair FAH-vor-reh) - A coffee, please
Un bicchiere di vino rosso/bianco (oon bee-KYEH-reh dee VEE-noh

ROHS-soh/BYAHN-koh) - A glass of red/white wine

Il conto, per favore (eel KOHN-toh, pair FAH-vor-reh) - The bill, please

Common Phrases:
Come stai? (KOH-meh stai) - How are you?
Molto bene, grazie (MOHL-toh BEH-neh, GRAH-tsyeh) - Very nicely, thank you
Mi chiamo... (mee KYAH-moh) - My name is...
Mi scusi, ne capisco (mee SKOO-zee, non kah-PEES-koh) - Excuse me, I don't understand

Farewells:
Arrivederci (ah-ree-veh-DEHR-chee) - Goodbye
A presto (ah PRES-toh) - See you shortly
Buona giornata (BWON-nah JOR-nah-tah) - Have a nice day

Learning and adopting these basic words will not only help you converse better but also show respect for the local culture and enrich your whole experience in Napoli. Buon viaggio! (Have a wonderful trip!)

Health and Safety Tips

Health and safety are critical issues for any tourist to Napoli. While the city offers a diverse cultural experience, taking basic precautions is essential for a safe and enjoyable stay. Here are some health and safety considerations for visiting Naples:

Stay Hydrated:
Napoli's Mediterranean climate may be hot and humid, especially in the summer. Carry a reusable water bottle and drink plenty of fluids to stay hydrated, especially if you'll be spending time outdoors or walking about the city.

Protect yourself from the Sun:
The sun in Napoli may be harsh, so wear sunscreen with a high SPF, sunglasses, and a wide-brimmed hat to protect your skin and eyes from harmful UV rays.

Maintain Personal Safety:
While Napoli is generally safe for tourists, it is essential to take common sense precautions to protect yourself and your belongings. Keep valuables secure, especially in congested areas, and be aware of pickpockets in tourist destinations.

Stay aware of Traffic:
Napoli's streets may be packed and chaotic, so use caution while crossing the street and be aware of your surroundings. Use designated crosswalks, obey traffic signals, and be aware of unexpected cars, especially while navigating narrow streets.

Be aware of your Step:
Napoli's ancient center is marked by cobblestone sidewalks and uneven paths, so wear sturdy, comfortable shoes with good traction to prevent slips and falls. Walking on steep or uneven terrain requires extra attention, particularly after rain.

Stay Aware of COVID-19 Guidelines:
Keep up to speed on any COVID-19 regulations and restrictions that may apply during your trip to Napoli. To reduce the risk of transmission, follow local health guidelines, wear a mask in crowded or indoor settings, maintain social distance, and wash your hands often.

Maintain Emergency Contact Information:
In case of a crisis, have a list of emergency contact numbers handy, such as local police, medical services, and your country's embassy or consulate. It's also a good idea to have a copy of your passport

and travel insurance information with you at all times.

Utilize Licenced Services:
To avoid conflicts while using transportation services such as taxis or ridesharing apps, be sure to choose licensed providers and agree on costs in advance. Stick with known suppliers and avoid getting rides from unlicensed drivers.

Observe Local Customs and Laws:
Familiarize oneself with local customs, traditions, and laws to avoid inadvertently causing offense or getting into legal trouble. Respect holy buildings, dress modestly when appropriate, and refrain from engaging in any illegal activities.

Trust your Instincts:
Finally, use your instincts and common sense. If a situation seems to be hazardous or uncomfortable, leave it immediately and seek help if necessary. Traveling with a companion or in a group may provide an extra layer of security. By taking these health and safety measures, you may have a relaxing and worry-free holiday in Napoli, immersing yourself in the city's rich culture, history, and gourmet delights while being safe and healthy. Have a safe journey!

Emergency Number

Having emergency contacts on hand is essential while visiting Napoli in case of unforeseen circumstances. Before visiting Napoli, make sure you have the following emergency contacts in mind:

Emergency Services: Emergency Number: 112 - Call the Italian emergency number, 112, to reach the police, fire department, and ambulance. In an emergency, dial 112 for prompt assistance.

Polizia (Police):
Emergency: 112 -
Non-Emergency: 113 - You may call the police at the non-emergency number 113 to report a crime or for non-emergency situations.

Medical and Ambulatory Services (Ambulanza):
Emergency Number: 112 - Dial 112 in case you need an ambulance due to an emergency. Assistance will be provided by emergency medical services sent to your location.

Pronto Soccorso Hospital Emergency Rooms:

For immediate medical attention in the event of a serious medical emergency or accident, go to the nearest hospital emergency room (Ospedale Cardarelli: +39 081 747 1111; Ospedale Policlinico: +39 081 590 1111).

Fire Department (Vigili del Fuoco): Emergency Number: 112 - Contact the fire department by calling the emergency number 112 in the event of a fire, including building fires or dangerous fire situations.

Polizia Turistica, or Tourist Police:
Via Medina, 46, 80133 Napoli NA, Italy - Phone: +39 081 794 7225 - Travellers in need of assistance with lost or stolen documents, tourist scams, or other travel-related issues may turn to the Tourist Police.

Consulate or Embassy:
Get assistance related to your home country from the consulate or embassy of your foreign nation in Italy if you're a non-citizen. When facing challenges like lost passports, legal issues, or urgent medical attention, they could provide assistance.

The Municipal Police (Polizia Municipale) may be reached at 081 795 7034. Concerns about public safety and city rules that are not emergencies may be assisted by local authorities, such as the municipal police.

Having these emergency contacts with you throughout your stay in Napoli is a smart idea, so put them in your phone or write them down. To ensure that you stay safe and prepared throughout your vacation, make sure you familiarize yourself with the emergency protocols and procedures in the area.

Interactions and Web Connections

Communication and internet access are required throughout your Naples trip to stay connected, explore the city, and receive critical information. Below is a list of your options for getting online and communicating in Naples:

Mobile Network service:
TIM, Vodafone, and Wind Tre, three of Italy's most well-known mobile network carriers, all provide excellent service in Naples. Prepaid SIM cards and a choice of phone plans with call, text, and data options are available.

Foreign Roaming:

Before you go for your vacation, talk to your home mobile provider about your overseas roaming options. Make sure you are informed of the data limits and fees associated with using your phone while abroad, since roaming may incur additional charges.

Public Wi-Fi:
Many cafés, restaurants, hotels, and public places in Naples provide free Wi-Fi to customers. You may either ask a member of staff for the Wi-Fi password or check for indications that it is accessible. While public Wi-Fi is convenient, use caution while accessing sensitive information, such as online banking, via public networks.

Internet Cafes:
Napoli still has internet cafes where you may pay to use computers and the internet, although they aren't as common as they used to be. These institutions are useful if you need access to a computer or printer during your visit.

Mi-Fis and Other Portable Wi-Fi Devices:
Renting a Mi-Fi or other portable Wi-Fi device provides an additional option for getting online. These devices allow you to connect several devices to a secure Wi-Fi network and are ideal for guests

who need constant internet access while exploring the city.

Data Roaming Packages:
Before you go, think about getting a data roaming package from your home mobile operator or a local SIM card with a data plan. Data roaming packages usually provide discounted prices to international tourists and enable access to high-speed data while abroad.

Language Translation Applications:
Language translation apps may help you overcome language barriers while conversing in Napoli. Apps like Google Translate and Microsoft Translator allow for real-time translation of text and audio, making it easier to speak with locals and tour the area.

Offline Maps:
Before your journey, get offline maps of Napoli using software such as Google Maps or Maps.me. Offline maps allow you to navigate the city without using data, which may be very useful if you find yourself in an area with bad network access.

Emergency Calls:

Remember that even if you don't have an active SIM card or mobile plan, you may still contact local authorities (police, ambulance, fire department) by dialing 112.

Using these communication options and internet access methods, you may stay connected, informed, and prepared while exploring Napoli's busy streets.

Useful Apps and Websites

When visiting Napoli, several useful apps and websites can improve your experience, help you explore the city, find local sights, and discover secret gems. Here are some must-have apps and websites for tourists in Napoli:

Google Maps (App/Web):
Google Maps is essential for exploring Napoli's streets, finding public transportation routes, identifying sites, and discovering nearby restaurants and shops. You can also download offline maps for places with limited internet connection.

Moovit (App):

Moovit offers real-time public transportation information, including bus, metro, and tram plans, routes, and expected arrival times. It's a great tool for planning your trips around Napoli using public transport.

Mytaxi (App):
Mytaxi allows you to book legal taxis in Napoli quickly and easily. You can watch your taxi's arrival in real-time, pay safely through the app, and rate your driver afterward.

Napoli Unplugged (Website):
Napoli Unplugged is a thorough website giving expert tips, guides, and suggestions for experiencing Napoli. It covers everything from ancient places and cultural draws to eating, shopping, and local events.

Napoli Official Tourism Website (Website):
The main tourism website of Napoli offers useful information for tourists, including city maps, sightseeing suggestions, event lists, and practical travel tips. It's a great resource for planning your trip to Napoli.

NapoliToday (Website):

NapoliToday is a local news website covering current events, cultural happenings, and living themes in Napoli. It's a useful resource for staying updated on what's going on during your visit.

Eat Napoli (App):
Eat Napoli is a food-focused app that helps you find the best restaurants, shops, and bars in Napoli. It features reviews, scores, and suggestions from locals and fellow tourists, making it easier to find real Neapolitan food.

Napoli WiFi (App):
Napoli WiFi is an app that helps you find free Wi-Fi hotspots throughout the city. It's useful for tourists who depend on internet access for conversation, transportation, or work while visiting Napoli.

Napoli Street Food (App):
Napoli Street Food is a handy app for foodies looking to explore Napoli's bustling street food scene. It offers information about popular street food sellers, neighborhood favorites, and must-try meals.

Airbnb Experiences (App/Web):

Airbnb Experiences offers unique, selected events and tours led by locals in Napoli. From food classes and guided walking tours to cultural lessons and outdoor adventures, you can discover real experiences suited to your interests.

With these apps and websites at your hands, you'll have all the tools you need to make the most of your time in Napoli, discover secret gems, and experience the city like a local.

CONCLUSION

After finishing our comprehensive travel guide to Napoli, it is clear that this city offers visitors a really unique experience because of its extraordinary beauty, extensive history, and vibrant culture. Whether a visitor is interested in art, history, gastronomy, or just the excitement of exploration, Napoli has plenty to offer, from its ancient ruins and historic sites to its internationally recognised cuisine and vibrant street life.

We've journeyed through Napoli's past and present in this book, revealing undiscovered gems, must-see attractions, and useful advice to ensure a smooth and enjoyable visit. We've explored the UNESCO-designated historic part of the city, where narrow lanes lead to expansive piazzas, exquisite cathedrals, and bustling markets. We've looked at masterpieces from the Renaissance to ancient artifacts at museums and galleries. We have sampled the culinary delights of Napoli, delighting in traditional dishes such as pizza, pasta, and seafood along with mouth watering street food specialties. We have also really enjoyed the vibrant street life of Napoli, where there is always something fresh to see, hear, or smell that stimulates the senses.

Napoli is a city with a soul, a place where passion, inventiveness, and resiliency come together, while its attractions and cuisine may not be overlooked. This city has weathered many storms throughout history, including wars, invasions, and natural disasters, yet it has persevered and continues to stand strong, welcoming visitors with open arms and a passion for life.

We welcome you to appreciate Napoli's contrasts and paradoxes, its chaos and charm, its historical roots and contemporary life as you get ready to explore it. Interact with its people, get fully immersed in its culture, and let its beauty and soul enchant you. Whether you stroll through its historic lanes, indulge in its delectable cuisine, or just take in the atmosphere at a neighborhood café, Napoli is sure to make a lasting impression on your heart and soul.

So prepare for an amazing trip to Napoli by packing your bags, tying up your walking shoes, and getting ready. Whatever your interests, history, art, cuisine, or just being a curious traveler looking for new experiences, Napoli welcomes you with open arms and is ready to enthrall, inspire, and enchant you at every turn. Che bello viaggio e benvenuto a Napoli! (travel safely, and I'll see you in Naples!)

Printed in Great Britain
by Amazon